Heart Vision

Tarot's Inner Path

Michael Orlando Yaccarino

Dedication

I came back into this world to find you,
Taken on this mantle of flesh to hold you,
So that we may never be parted again.

As always and in everything, this book is devoted to SDR with a love beyond words and one unbounded by time.

Heart Vision
Tarot's Inner Path

Michael Orlando Yaccarino

Foreword by Rachel Pollack

Afterword by Normandi Ellis

Illustrations by Scot D. Ryersson,
Gary Lund, and David Palladini

Copyright © 2018 Michael Orlando Yaccarino

First edition 2018

All rights reserved. No part of this work may be reproduced or utilized in any form by any means, electronic or mechanical, including *xerography, photocopying, microfilm,* and *recording,* or by any information storage system without permission in writing from the publishers.

Every effort was made to obtain permission to reproduce material in this book. If any proper acknowledgment has not been included, we encourage copyright holders to notify the publishers.

Illustrations Credits

Scot D. Ryersson: all interior illustrations unless otherwise indicated © by the artist. Gary Lund: front-cover art © by the artist. David Palladini: back-cover art and Egyptian study (Afterword) © by the artist.

Published by
Mandrake of Oxford
PO Box 250
OXFORD
OX1 1AP (UK)

Printed on acid free paper certification from three leading environmental organizations: the Forest Stewardship Council™ (FSC®), the Sustainable Forestry Initiative® (SFI®) and the Programme for the Endorsement of Forestry Certification (PEFC™)

Contents

Foreword by Rachel Pollack	7
Introduction	11

Heart Vision — 15
From Game Playing to Higher Wisdom — 16
Experiencing Heart Vision — 21
Transformation through Synthesis — 25
Looking at the Cards — 27

Seventy Eight Stations — 34
The Major Arcana — 35
The Fool — 40
The Magician — 42
The High Priestess — 44
The Empress — 46
The Emperor — 48
The Hierophant — 50
The Lovers — 52
The Chariot — 54
Strength — 56
The Hermit — 58
The Wheel of Fortune — 60
Justice — 62
The Hanged Man — 64
Death — 66
Temperance — 68
The Devil — 70
The Tower — 72
The Star — 74
The Moon — 76
The Sun — 78
Judgement — 80
The World — 82

The Minor Arcana	84
Wands	90
Cups	111
Swords	138
Pentacles	162
The Inner Path	188
Finding the Way	189
Preparing for the Inner Path	191
Determining the Route	195
Shuffling and Cutting the Cards	196
Reversals	197
Spreads and Spread Positions	199
Assessment (1-card spread)	203
Imbalance I.D. (2-card spread)	205
Present-Past-Future (3-card spread)	210
Trend Flow (4-card spread)	217
Crossroads (5-card spread)	221
Arch Bride (5-card spread)	231
Guidance (6-card spread)	235
Heart of the Matter (6-card spread)	241
Soul of the Matter (6-card spread)	252
Where All Paths Meet	257
Returning to the Open Road	258
Intuitive Knowing	259
Beyond the Inner Path	265
Afterword by Normandi Ellis	267
Thankful Remembrance	269
Select Bibliography and Suggested Reading	271
About the Author	274
About the Contributors	275
Index	278

Foreword
by Rachel Pollack

To begin, a little history. In the early 1960s, Tarot was an obscure subject, described in dense occult writings, with complex diagrams and concepts largely inaccessible to people not already trained in esoteric doctrines. And then there were the fortune tellers who would warn of terrible dangers, or promise marvelous discoveries. Then a woman named Eden Gray created a series of short books aimed at beginners, yet informed by a deep knowledge of occult tradition. In a speech in Chicago when she was ninety six, Gray said that she had been running an esoteric bookstore, and when people asked for a good beginner's book on Tarot there just wasn't any, so she decided to do it herself.

Many of us from that time discovered the Tarot through Eden Gray. Later we would go on to more complex studies, deeper approaches. Or so we thought. A number of years ago I began to look at the meanings so many of us had come to see as standard for the various cards, and I discovered something strange. When I examined the writings of Arthur Edward Waite, designer of the deck used in this book, I often did not find the ideas I assumed had come from him. Nor did they appear in other older commentators. A little bit of searching and I found that over and over the meanings I and many others had taken for traditional in fact came from Eden Gray. She did not change the older interpretations so much as add new possibilities, new layers of ideas.

I don't think Michael Orlando Yaccarino will mind my beginning this foreword by invoking Eden Gray. Like Gray, Michael has studied the Tarot with dedication and sensitivity. And like Gray he has given us short vivid descriptions of each card that gives us a sense of what we are seeing when we lay the cards on the table, without narrowing our own response to the pictures.

Since the early 1960s when Eden Gray brought the Tarot into modern consciousness the ways we look at the cards have greatly expanded, becoming, among other things, more psychological. Michael builds on this way of doing Tarot. For example (literally chosen at random), he tells us of the Two of Wands' "Veiled Aspects," that "such a mindset can degrade into one of unrelenting obsession and perpetual dissatisfaction."

At the same time, he remembers that Tarot is above all a *visual* medium, pictures with no original texts but only a long history of interpretation. Thus, of that same veiled Two of Wands he comments, "Recalling the suit's association with fire, the red cap implies an explosive temper intolerant of those unable to react with the same enthusiasm toward his interests." This is fanciful, for there are no other people in the card, and yet it comes through a subtle visual clue connected to the Tarot's traditional structure, in which each of the four suits belongs to one of the four medieval elements of Fire, Water, Air, and Earth.

In the early 1980s I described my own approach to Tarot as "loving the images," returning again and again to the pictures, seeing them as much as possible with fresh eyes instead of fixed meanings. Michael exhibits this kind of sensitivity and freshness. With the Five of Swords (again, chosen at random) he writes, "Rare among any of the Tarot's largely impassive figures is a discernible facial expression...One interpretation might describe it as the satisfied smirk of a battle's victor while gloating at the losers' retreat." And more, "maybe this is why the furthest figure appears hunched over in dazed disbelief."

Like Eden Gray, Michael Orlando Yaccarino uses the Rider deck of Waite and Pamela Colman Smith (known to her many admirers as "Pixie"). Some have suggested that it was Gray's books that made the Rider the world standard for Tarot decks. I doubt it. As much as I respect Gray's work, Pixie's drawings carry the special quality of inviting us in, showing us moments that open up entire stories. Michael has entered those stories and invites us to discover them with him, sometimes offering us new tales. Of the Six of Wands he writes, "An alternative interpretation might view the central figure as a clever philanderer receiving the simultaneous adulation of his many, if perhaps unwitting, conquests."

Some people believe beginners in Tarot should not consider doing any readings until they have memorized all the meanings. In my experience, readings are the very process of learning. I began to read the cards as soon as I got them, deck in one hand, book—Eden Gray, of course—in the other. Like many others I learned what the cards meant through practice. Most important, I learned that meanings change, expand, even mutate through the process of trying to figure out what they are telling us. I have not asked Michael but I suspect that his idea of the Six of Wands as a multiple philanderer might very well have emerged in a particular reading.

In one of my favorite parts of this book Michael describes Tarot readings as an "art form." No matter how many interpretations or symbolic systems we learn, it is all theory until the cards come up in a reading. It is just because reading is a kind of art, akin perhaps most of all to story-telling, that new meanings can appear to us at any moment. Art dies when it becomes repetitious. Michael reminds us that habit and ritual may help us enter the creative moment, but we also should do things differently at times, just to open ourselves to new possibilities.

Most art requires structure, such as the chords that underlie popular songs. In Tarot readings, spreads help us get a sense of what the reading is about. Instead of just a scattering of cards on the table we get to see each card as the answer to a particular question. Michael takes this a step further, suggesting particular approaches to the different groups of cards, the Majors, Courts, Aces, and Pips.

No one would expect to learn how to write novels without ever reading any. As it happens I teach creative writing, and a good part of my work involves suggesting books for students to read that will inspire their own work. So Michael gives the apprentice reader-artist sample self-readings of the spreads he describes, showing how one artist works with the pictures to create a story of one's own life in a particular moment. He shows us, in the best way, by demonstration, how to combine the cards, noticing, for example, that three figures might appear in each picture in a reading.

Many people learning Tarot find that the hardest thing to grasp is the way cards work together in a reading. They can figure out what each card might mean by itself but find it hard to create an overall pattern, a story. As he goes through the varied spreads he offers us, Michael suggests possible "connections" between the cards in their different positions, asking for example, "In what ways do these cards oppose or reinforce each other?" or "What does the Shadow reveal about the hidden nature of the Key aspect?"

What is the mark of a good beginner's book? Simple, that people who are not beginners can learn from it. And this we find again and again in this work of distilled simplicity.

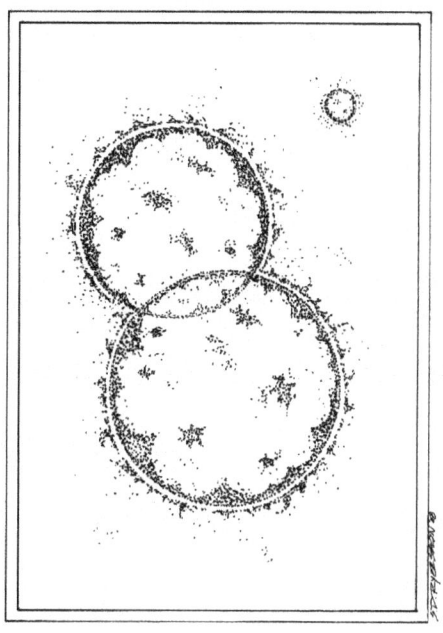

Introduction

The Tarot offers a gallery of possibilities to be examined, absorbed, and lived. The greater part of this guide is devoted to utilizing the cards as a solitary oracular instrument. You will also find suggested card interpretations and simple yet powerful spreads, many illumined by real-life self-readings.[1] This work is not meant to be a definitive one on the subject in any way. Instead, what is offered here is a perspective capable of expanding and deepening your experience of this incomparable divinatory gateway.

This book will focus on solitary reading—a process capable of

---

1 Unless specified otherwise, the terms reader and self-reader, and similarly, reading and self-reading will be used interchangeably throughout this work.

producing a multi-dimensional snapshot. In this way, the cards capture many aspects of such a moment so one may study them in numerous ways. As for the majority of us who become either detoured or lost on life's journey, a self-reading can help regain our bearings. Moreover, it can suggest alternate routes to an inner path where revelation, understanding, and profound transformation can be found.

Before we begin, allow me to share an intimate moment on the genesis of my own relationship with the cards. My initial acquaintance with the Tarot was made through the first deck I ever owned—the Aquarian Tarot obtained from a local bookshop when I was twelve years old. The glorious beauty of David Palladini's artistry has not only retained its considerable power since I first discovered it in the mid-1970s, but has only deepened with the passage of time. Similarly, I acquired *The Windows of Tarot* by F.D. Graves, published in 1973 as a guide to accompany this deck. Astutely describing the Tarot as "a look at life," this slim volume contains a treasury of evocative statements which set my budding novice's heart aflame, such as: "Within this body of knowledge, we may discover the immutable nature of our inner selves, a guide to chart our paths along the cosmic shore, and even a language of words unsaid and dreams unrealised."[2] I recall quite vividly studying the book whilst in the parked family car outside the Roman Catholic grammar school I attended at that time. Still cherished in my personal library, almost the entirety of the text is passionately marked throughout with yellow and blue highlighter by my young hand. Several of its pages remain adhered together with melted candlewax from some forgotten session. Nonetheless, what was it which led me initially to the "occult" section of the bookshop where I found these catalytic gate-openers?

---

2   F.D. Graves, *The Windows of Tarot* (Dobbs Ferry, 1973).

I spent the first twelve years of my life in a house constructed sometime in the 1920s. While the suburban Northeastern United States town in which it was located was fairly unremarkable, the persistent apparently paranormal occurrences experienced in that home were far from common. Fortunately, I attribute an innately inquisitive mind and a stable family environment as instrumental in my view on these happenings as more an adventure than an unwanted ordeal. Perhaps being born a middle child upon both an Astrological cusp and seasonal equinox has blessed me with feet planted typically—if somewhat precariously—between realms anyway. To be sure, some of these still inexplicable otherworldly encounters have left me perplexed, but no less intrigued with a desire to understand them.

Among all of these moments, there is one in particular perhaps most unforgettable for its still-evolving meaningfulness and lasting sense of wonder. It took place one summer afternoon in a room suffused with warmth and sunlight. All around me, luminous spheres began to slowly appear to drift through the air in an unhurried fashion. Vividly-colored tendrils wavered electrically within each one as they floated by languidly. I felt no fear of any kind. On the contrary, they filled me with gratefulness, both heartfelt and pure, for this direct communication. As I write this now, I am ever thankful for this opportunity in which the invisible revealed itself so splendidly.

Even so, oftentimes in the past, I longed for the spheres to repeat their ephemeral dance since that childhood encounter. The passing of so many moons on my journey were required for me to comprehend how in fact, they have never truly departed. I know now the spheres' original appearance blessed my young eyes in the way they did before adulthood concerns might block my open reception of them. So I make efforts each day to exist in the present by remaining free from such useless obstructions as past regret and future worry. When I am blessed by succeeding in this continuing challenge, the vision returns effortlessly—only now transformed.

For the spheres accompany me as I wander a stunning stretch of surf and sand while feeling at one with the spirit of that ever-changing tide. They comprise the tear I attempt and happily fail to control whenever enthralled by a moving musical composition, artwork, or film. They resound in my sigh of contentment upon tasting a favorite dish. They are present each time a Tarot self-contemplation encourages me toward some desired change or understanding. They exist in a needed touch, either given or received. And in the gentlest whisper, they speak through the rhythmic drumming of cool rain against a windowpane as I drift into dream.

So then, what was given me from this childhood marvel? Today, I accept it as both a greeting from and an affirmation of those realms seemingly beyond, but intrinsically part of everyday existence. Those shimmering spheres have become the guide-lights along my own path. I trust them implicitly since they directed me to, among other fruitful explorations, the Tarot itself. These seventy-eight cards have nourished my spirit as most assuredly they will your own.

Do I know in what form these radiant guardians will manifest themselves or to which station along the path they will bring me next? *I feel not compelled to know.* But I am eager to find out—for illumination in all its shades and colors will surely follow.

I
Heart Vision

I walk about stars. I sail the heavens with gods. I hold long conversations with beings of light. I am a mind afire. I am the sun from noon to dusk, heat of the day, blaze of sunset.
—Normandi Ellis, *Awakening Osiris: A New Translation of the Egyptian Book of the Dead*[3]

---

3   Normandi Ellis, *Awakening Osiris: A New Translation of the Egyptian Book of the Dead* (Grand Rapids, 1988).

From Game Playing to Higher Wisdom

The history of today's popular oracle, meditation, and self-help decks is linked to that of the more well-known Tarot. To be sure, the genesis of the latter is characterized by frequent misconception and factual error. The persistence and misinterpretation of colorful theories by 18th- and 19th-century occultists[4] combined with faulty historical research have generated these. Fortunately, contemporary findings have uncovered the cards' perhaps far less outwardly occult, although just as intriguing beginnings.

First devised in 9th-century China, game-playing cards reached Western Europe from the Islamic world after modification in India and Persia. The earliest still-existing Tarot cards were lavishly custom-made and hand-painted by 15th-century artists for game playing by the Italian nobility. Current research supports the existence of decks prior to these—both more opulent ones for royal play in other courts, most notably

---

4   Aleister Crowley (The Master Therion), *The Book of Thoth* (York Beach, 2000). The work's authorship was attributed to The Master Therion, one of Crowley's mystical names, when published originally in 1944. While praising the scholarship of Éliphas Lévi (1810-1875; born Alphonse Louis Constant) in it, the trailblazing Crowley charges such noted occultists as Jean-Baptiste Alliette or "Etteilla" (1738-1791), Joséphin Péladan (1858-1918), Oswald Wirth (1860-1943), and P.D. Ouspensky (1878-1947) as guilty in their Tarot systems of ignorant verbosity and slavish mimicry "…to the conventional Mediaeval designs. (Their luck was out: the Tarot is a razor!)"

5   Jereer El-Moor [Gerald Elmore], "The Occult Tradition of the Tarot in Tangency with Ibn 'Arabi's Life and Teachings," (Berkeley and Oxford, 2002). In this article, the author attempts to establish the Tarot's provenance to the Near East and specifically 11th-century Egypt.

France, and those cruder in composition printed inexpensively for the masses—examples of which have simply not endured.[5] The word "tarot" is the French name for the Italian *Tarocchi*, a forerunner of such modern-day trick-taking card games as pinochle and bridge.

While first practiced in Italy, Cartomancy or card reading was not developed fully until the 18th century in France. Since this time, card reading has been established as a reliable divinatory tool of major and enduring significance. Generally, divination implies obtaining hidden knowledge, quite often of future events, by interpreting observable omens or those purposely caused to happen. Cartomancy falls into the latter category since it typically involves the deliberate drawing of cards, even if done so randomly. Detailed information on early card reading techniques is scant at best. Nevertheless, with powerfully evocative images nearly universal in archetypal content, the Tarot and related decks have proven sturdy enough to withstand adaptation to a myriad of artistic styles and for a multitude of reading practices. Author and mage Paul Huson touches upon the multidimensional mysteries applicable to both card reading for others or the self:

> Cards can in effect be seen as tools for reflecting matters hidden deep within the unconscious minds of those who consult them. They appear to function in ways similar to the ambiguous illustrations employed in projective psychological tests, whereby

---

[6] Paul Huson, correspondence with author, August 2016. Musician, artist, and magician, Jan Fries defines the Deep Mind (or deep mind) as "deeper aspects of Self"; these can include: the "gods," "spirits," "angels and demons," "beast totems," "allies," and the "subconscious mind"—"all words meant to describe specific aspects of a single phenomenon, of which the conscious self is but another aspect." Learn more in the following book: Jan Fries, *Visual Magick: A Manual of Freestyle Shamanism* (Oxford, 1992).

the images are spun into revelatory narratives that may discover underlying motives, concerns, and ways of perceiving society and the world. Factor into this process the psi powers of the Deep Minds of both the card reader and the consultant and the range of perception in theory becomes almost limitless.[6]

Oracle decks first appeared in 18th-century France, a related outgrowth of the venerable Tarot. Their most well-documented proponent was Madame Lenormand,[7] celebrated French cartomancer to European royalty of the time. Oracle decks proliferated in the latter 20th century and continue to flourish in the new millennium. Varying widely in style and typically not as strictly structured as the Tarot, oracle cards can be employed to ascertain higher wisdom for the solitary reader or the same for others. Cards can serve equally well as a focus for contemplation through which awareness is expanded, as evidenced by the wealth of self-help decks available today.

Arthur Edward Waite,[8] the early 20th-century occultist, guided artist Pamela Colman Smith[9] in her creation of the pictures for an innovative Tarot deck. William Rider & Son of London first published it in 1909. Certain teachings of the Hermetic Order of the Golden Dawn, a magical

---

7 Marie-Anne Adélaïde Lenormand (or Le Normand) was born in Alençon, France in 1772 and died in Paris, France in 1843.
8 Arthur Edward Waite was born in 1857 in Brooklyn, New York and died in London, England in 1942.
9 Pamela Colman Smith, also known as Pixie, was born in London, England in 1878 and died in Bude, Cornwall, England in 1951.
10 Nearly a decade later, Arthur Edward Waite commissioned artist John B. Trinick to create twenty-three Tarot images for private use by The Fellowship of the Rosy Cross, a mystical organization he founded in 1915 descended from the Hermetic Order of the Golden Dawn which had disbanded earlier. Learn more in the following book: Tali Goodwin and Marcus Katz, *Abiding in the Sanctuary: The Waite-Trinick Tarot 1917-1923* (Keswick, 2011).

society to which both Waite and Colman Smith belonged, influenced the specific symbols used and their arrangement in the images.[10] Tarot author and authority on the women of the Golden Dawn, Mary K. Greer elucidates the artist's significant contribution:

> Who knows what Tarot would be like today without Pamela Colman Smith's artistry? Unarguably, she created the most influential deck design ever, not only in its original art, but in how it has inspired subsequent deck creators and authors for several vital reasons. The faux-medieval scenes of the Minor Arcana naturally evoke a storytelling urge and encourage rich psychological projection, yet the stories always seem to reflect the essential meanings of the cards. The ambiguous expressions on many of the faces allow for flexible interpretations of the emotions and sentiments portrayed. And despite the figures being Caucasian in appearance and median in size, there is a feeling of diversity with an equal number of masculine and feminine figures, including several with characteristics of both. Pamela Colman Smith had a rare ability to step between the world we see and the world we do not to bring back that timeless essence found in all great works of art.[11]

Counted among the varied branches of esoteric knowledge studied by the Golden Dawn that helped shape the Rider-Waite[12] deck were the Kabbalah, Freemasonry, Rosicrucianism, Numerology, Astrology, and Alchemy, among others.[13] However, a comprehensive understanding of

---

11   Mary K. Greer, correspondence with author, October 2016.
12   Many refer to this pack as the Rider-Waite-Smith deck in an effort to recognize Colman Smith's undeniable contribution to its long-lasting usability and aesthetic beauty.
13   Mogg Morgan, *Tankhem: Seth and Egyptian Magick* (Oxford, 2005).
14   From an edition reproducing its original 1909 coloring to those simply inspired by it, the Rider-Waite Tarot deck is readily available worldwide in a variety of forms in several languages.

how the cards' symbols relate to these occult systems is not mandatory for the learner to use this pack quite successfully.

The Rider-Waite Tarot[14] is the mode of transportation for our journey. Clearly, this particular deck enjoys an undeniable popularity. Easily obtainable worldwide, it continues to shape innumerable variant ones produced since its debut more than a century ago.[15] As already noted, the genuine depth and beguiling artistry of the Rider-Waite Tarot has assured its worthiness as a source for continued study and use in our new millennium. This book contains several key original illustrations designed to illuminate the text. Their purpose is to emphasize essential symbolic elements of the Tarot, those essential to the Rider-Waite deck and other packs, as well as mystical truths beyond the limitations of time and place.

Not surprisingly, close similarities exist between standard playing card deck structure and that of the subsequently devised Tarot. While the following structure applies directly to the Rider-Waite cards, formation between Tarot decks can vary considerably. In brief, two distinct components comprise the deck's seventy-eight cards. These include: the Major Arcana ("arcana" being Latin for "enigmas" or "mysteries") or Trumps, consisting of twenty-one numbered cards; and the Minor Arcana, consisting of fifty six cards subdivided into four suits—Wands, Cups, Swords, and Pentacles. Each of these suits contains four Court cards (King, Queen, Knight, and Page) and ten numbered "Pip"[16]

---

15 Artist David Palladini's Aquarian Tarot referenced earlier in this book is an example of such a variant deck.

16 The term "Pip" used to identify Tarot cards Ace through Ten of the Minor Arcana is related to the deck's earliest incarnation as a game-playing device, similar in use as standard playing cards, dice, and dominoes, all which use simple dot-like markings to identify their value—these resembling fruit pits or pips.

cards (Ace through Ten). Finally, there is The Fool card given the value of zero and often assigned a position preceding the twenty-one Major Arcana cards. The Fool enjoys a separate existence as a universal representative upon a philosophical quest to understand the self and the universe.

In this guide, we will recognize the cards as a viable way to visually transmit information of an elevated nature. The beneficial results received by several centuries of seekers who have gained insight through card reading verify this assertion. More than one form of mysticism[17] has proclaimed the heart as the very locus of the soul.[18] And it is the heart of the solitary viewer from which messages of guidance originate.

For whatever purpose one utilizes the cards, these images are most potently received with an open heart welcoming revelation. In truth, these images are perfectly capable of unexpected transformations. The paper borders separating the cards from each other, *as well as from you*, are deceptive at best—just an indefinite play of the light.

Experiencing Heart Vision

Advancement on any path takes place through efforts made along it. Perhaps ultimately this progress is of more value than reaching the actual goal itself. Yet an inherent contradiction ever taunts those on the quest

---

17 British author on spirituality, Evelyn Underhill (1875-1941) defines mysticism as "…the art of union with Reality. The mystic is a person who has attained that union in greater or less degree; or who aims at and believes in such attainment." Learn more in the following book: Evelyn Underhill, *Practical Mysticism: A Little Book for Normal People* (New York, 2006).

18 This belief is especially prevalent in the spirituality of Ancient Egypt and that of the Sufis, thus the inclusion of a variety of references to these mystical paths throughout this work.

toward greater understanding. For as awareness expands, vistas of unknowing open ever wider before us. One way these dimly-lit dimensions can be explored effectively is by both focused contemplation and illuminated intuitive knowing sparked through the art of divination.

By definition, a mosaic is made by setting small, colored pieces of stone, tile, or glass into a surface to form a picture or decorative design. The fascinating etymology of this art term is associated with the Greek word *mouseios*, relating to the inspirational Muses of that ancient culture, as well as to Moses, the biblical intermediary between man and the heavens. Surely, the realms of the artist and this biblical celestial liaison intersect in reliance upon intuition. Revealing the unseen through pictures, one of the potential benefits of contemplative self-reading is the development of and confidence in this seemingly ephemeral capacity.

If we define divination as accessing hidden information—card reading being just one of its many forms—intuition is the ability to achieve such without immediately apparent methods. Sufi teacher Irina Tweedie[19] quoted her spiritual master as stating, "Knowledge comes through the heart. From the heart to the mind."[20] While intellectual wisdom can be distorted by appearances, well-balanced intuition, referred to here as heart vision, sees into the essence or inner reality—that which is typically undetected, discounted, or not fully perceived by the five

---

19 Irina Tweedie (born Irina Tamara Karpow) was born in Russia and died in 1999.

20 Irina Tweedie, *Daughter of Fire: A Diary of a Spiritual Training with a Sufi Master* (Grass Valley, 1986) offers a detailed autobiographical account of the 20th-century, Russian-born mystic's spiritual training in India. In *Sufi Teachings: The Smiling Forehead* (London, 1996), Hazrat Inayat Khan defines the heart as "…the depth of the mind, the mind being the surface of the heart."

senses. Mystic and spiritual teacher, Reshad Feild[21] describes the aim of this expanded perception: "If we can see the world as it really is, we can see the perfect patterns behind it…We can see this if we are awake."[22] When intuition is used in divination selflessly to benefit others, it can be an uplifting experience. The 10th-century Persian Sufi writer Abû Bakr al-Kalâbâdhî notes, "[Ecstasy] is the hearing and sight of the heart."[23] Unfortunately, 20th-century fabricators of sensationalist fiction and film have promoted the image of the card reader skilled at both predicting specific, future happenings whilst delivering a sinister cackle on cue. Instead, those reading the cards are challenged to accept and trust the illumination received with objectivity and confidence.

We all experience instances of heart vision. Everyday life is filled with those moments when we simply *know*, with unshakable conviction, that the right conclusion has been uncovered. At the essence of each of these, a series of profound connections or micro-decisions are made leading to deeper wisdom—toward more fully grasping that which is outwardly unknown. Orin channeled by Sanaya Roman explains:

> Intuition is the ability to know without words, to sense the truth without explanations. Intuition operates beyond time and space; it is a link to your higher self. Intuition is not bound by the physical body. It operates knowing that past, present and future are simultaneous, happening in the "now" moment. It is the voice of your innermost self, your soul, which is always looking out for you.[24]

---

21 Reshad Feild (born Richard Timothy Feild) was born in Hascombe, England in 1934 and died in Devon, England in 2016.
22 Reshad Feild, *The Alchemy of the Heart* (Dorset, 1990).
23 Abû Bakr al-Kalâbâdhî, *The Doctrine of the Sufis* (Lahore, 1966).
24 Sanaya Roman, *Personal Power through Awareness: A Guidebook for Sensitive People* (Novato, 1986).

The work of the card reader is not to be definitively *correct* in the limiting definition of that term. For most of us, much of life is navigating through vast grey zones of vague implication. Author on Paganism and Druidry, Nimue Brown notes:

> Uncertainty is incredibly liberating…We are surrounded by mystery. Life and consciousness are mysteries. Death is a mystery. As soon as we try to fit the many mysteries into tidy little stories, we strip the numinous from them. Facing the enormity of all that we do not know, is a far more exciting proposition.[25] Divination does not take the mystery or uncertainty out of life. It gives you more room to explore the possibilities that the inevitable mysteries and uncertainties create. If we let it, sitting down with a Tarot pack, or a Rune set can be an act of facing the enormities of life. Open hearted, open minded, waiting to see if the universe wants to share something, and then figuring out what to do with whatever is shared. It is a strange, creative process, but an enriching one.[26]

The process of effective card reading works by drawing light toward such areas of uncertainty. And while every session cannot yield stunning examples of intuitive brilliance, each can result in a sliver of finely-colored glass to be applied to a greater mosaic of fuller understanding and practical options. Visionary artist Gary Lund explains how oracular cards "offer a focus point we respond to—to open us to greater possibilities, to clarify the present moment we find ourselves in. Stillness within movement."[27]

The heart as the organ of inner-knowing plays a crucial role in a reading. Opening our hearts to receive intuited wisdom or revealed

---

[25] Nimue Brown, *Spirituality without Structure: The Power of Finding Your Own Path* (Winchester, 2013).

[26] Nimue Brown, correspondence with author, September 2016.

[27] Gary Lund, interview by Michael Orlando Yaccarino, "Moving Stillness: A Moment with Visionary Artist Gary Lund," *Tarosophist International*, 2010, vol. 1, issue 6:5.

knowledge is highly demanding. For it necessitates technical prowess gained through that which there are no substitutes—real practice, life experience, and self-reflection.

Feats of stunning intuition can impress. Yet they are largely worthless unless received with some form of useful guidance to assist in positive transformation. Real divination is not a party game. As implied by the word itself—from the Latin *divinus* ("of god")—at the essence of this practice is an attempt to reveal hidden realities. As such, one's motivations for undertaking it should ideally be of a respectful nature. Humbleness is required in this art. How could it be otherwise if we view the process as a way to the inner path? Founder of The Clan of Tubal Cain, Robert Cochrane (Roy Bowers)[28] notes, "All mystical thought is based upon one major premise: the realization of truth as opposed to illusion. The student of the 'mysteries' is essentially a searcher after truth, or as the ancient traditions described it, 'Wisdom.'"[29]

Transformation through Synthesis

Before a closer look at the individual cards, it would be helpful to at least provide a cursory discussion of a concept reverberating significantly throughout almost all of the Major Arcana, and perhaps more subtlety, across the Minor Arcana as well. As already noted, the Tarot first developed most fully in Renaissance Italy. As a whole, its densely symbolic imagery is a testament to the cross-fertilization of secular, sacred, and mystical influences characterizing the ideas of this flourishing

---

28 Robert Cochrane (born Roy Bowers) was born in London, England in 1931 and died in Slough, Berkshire, England in 1966.
29 Cochrane's (Bowers') ardent quest for Truth and Wisdom may be explored in the following book: Shani Oates, ed., *The Star Crossed Serpent III: 'The Taper That Lights the Way'* (Oxford, 2016).

age. Among them were the religious beliefs and philosophical theories known as Hermeticism. In 15th-century Italy where a structured Tarot first emerged, this system was regaining popularity following many centuries of disapproval for its unorthodox approaches. This may have been so since chief among them was a thoroughly optimistic belief in the human ability to accomplish union with the Divine through enlightenment—and without need of the clergy as intermediary. A series of wisdom texts[30] attributed to Hermes Trismegistus ("Thrice-Greatest Hermes") preserved these sacred teachings originating in ancient Egypt. This mythical scribe is associated with the Egyptian deity Thoth and the Grecian god Hermes, perhaps a unification of the two. The earthly vehicle of the work was a group of divinely-inspired pagan Hellenistic-Egyptian writers.

One of the key concepts of the Hermetic tradition is the recognition of duality. In its simplest form, Hermetic Dualism assumes the coexistence of two opposing principles or forces within existence. These categories can include such culturally specific notions as the finite and the infinite, the earthly and the celestial, the genders, as well as many other less distinct dichotomies. Comprised of matter and spirit, Hermeticism views the human condition as the ultimate container of these dualistic energies. An expansion of this thinking implies how portions of differing elements may actually reside in the other. Moreover, the transcendence of duality's limitations happens through a complete understanding and acceptance of its components. According to some beliefs, the attainment of this transformative goal is achievable only through union with the Divine. This process results in the synthesis of opposites and the deification of the individual. Variations on this basic

---

30 These 2nd- and 3rd-century AD Greco-Latin works are known as the *Hermetica*.

idea began as far back as primitive religious practice, its presence already fully manifested in the complexities of ancient Egyptian cosmology and Mexican shamanism, and its most salient features evident in the early foundations of almost all major world religions surviving to the present day.

The purposeful use of specific symbols and image composition expressing Dualism in early Tarot deck design attest to the resurgence of Hermetic ideas in 15th-century Italy. The following card-by-card examination discusses key instances in which the concept of Dualism survives in the Rider-Waite deck—shaped by Golden Dawn teachings. Although not crucial, an awareness of these particular symbols will intensify understanding of the cards' overall messages. Through them is conveyed one of the Tarot's most profound dualistic teachings—conflict and resolution reside in the same place. A transformative Tarot experience takes place when one embraces both to move beyond them.

Looking at the Cards

Tarot cards are instruments of revelation. Even so, we must remember how they are fashioned from the simplest of substances—nothing more than humble paper adorned with beguiling imagery. Yet to be sure, something extremely unique happens when surrendering to their messages through the eyes of the heart.

Upon discovering the extraordinary world of the Tarot, many novices overwhelm themselves in an attempt to absorb all that is available on the subject as quickly as possible. This is not only an impossible task, but also one with the potentially unfavorable result of thoroughly confusing the beginner.

The Tarot is a massive, multi-cultural, cross-disciplinary subject incorporating art, science, and the numinous—and happily, one worthy of a lifetime's devotion. It is also a topic inherently replete with both thought-provoking debate and frustrating contradiction. Therefore, in conjunction with the focus of this book, neither heavily detailed symbolic explanations, nor lists of correspondences for the cards are included here. Correspondences refer to associations between specific cards and aspects of an extensive variety of esoteric systems.[31]

Experts and amateurs continually debate the use of correspondences with the Tarot. In actuality, certain occultists made these associations with the cards only many years after the deck's original development. Consequently, some maintain how such systems unnecessarily confound the student as to the cards' genuine ancestry and symbolic content. At the same time, others avow their use as fundamental in the process of deciphering a reading. However, the opinion here does not view their inclusion as rigidly obligatory early on in card reading experience. It is suggested instead to become acquainted with correspondences after a thorough understanding of Tarot basics are first gained. Then the informed amateur can make the choice of including them or not in working with the cards.

Attributed to Confucius,[32] we are all familiar with the proverb "a picture is worth a thousand words." One of the essential lessons this book offers is to *look* to the cards and their observable relationships to each other for the most significant messages. Referring to the deck as a "visual tool," artist David Palladini reminds us how, "the original purpose

---

31 These systems and associations include, but are not limited to: Kabbalah, the Tree of Life, Gematria (alphanumeric decoding), Astrology, Zodiac, Numerology, Alchemy, Chakras, Runes, I Ching, colors, stones, deities, plants, animals, and even musical notes, body parts, and scents.

32 Confucius was born in 551 BC in the State of Lu, China where he died in 479 BC.

of illustration was actually 'illumination,' which in that context meant 'casting light' for those who could not read...Beautiful illuminations in religious texts transported the readers into another, higher place. So the original purpose of illustration was as a way of teaching through images."[33] An understanding of the Tarot's vivacious images joined with focused contemplation upon them can yield much more than the slavish memorization of charts and lists sometimes recommended for the novice.

In diverse spiritual teachings, great emphasis is placed upon the ability to maintain a poised position between the countless extremes of life. So accordingly and as will be seen, one of the predominant functions of the self-reading is its use in ascertaining sources of internal imbalance. The Mother of Modern Witchcraft, Doreen Valiente[34] reminds us in her sacred poetry, "If that which you seek, you find not within yourself, you will never find without."[35] Very often, imbalance manifests itself in disparities between your inner realm of feelings, thoughts, and motivations and the outer realm of responses to and interactions with a multiplicity of others and commonplace situations. Such generally experienced imbalances have the potential to form repetitive patterns impeding growth. Upon their identification, the cards can then be used to propose options capable of shaping these areas of concern toward

---

33 David Palladini, interview by Michael Orlando Yaccarino, "Sage of Aquarius: David Palladini and the Art of Being," *Tarosophist International*, 2009, vol. 1, issue 5:23. See the same article for a detailed exploration of the artist's Tarot-related work.

34 Doreen Valiente was born in London, England in 1922 and died in Brighton, England in 1999.

35 Doreen Valiente, *The Charge of the Goddess: The Poetry of Doreen Valiente* (Brighton, 2014).

that which is optimal. Ignoring such stumbling blocks—from mundane to cosmic—will hinder further progress the same beneficial goal.

Speaking on the work of an ancient poet who achieved spiritual profundity through deceptively commonplace language, the Sufi mystic Hazrat Inayat Khan[36] explains, "Within the outer cover was the true inner form."[37] Accordingly, while the Tarot can render visible the hidden aspects of our existence, it contains more than a few images of everyday life. The seemingly humdrum should never be dismissed lightly, for these everyday scenes point toward greater truths.

In his groundbreaking work on the Tarot, *The Book of Thoth*, occultist and ceremonial magician Aleister Crowley views the cards as both "living individuals" with whom the reader establishes relationships, as well as hieroglyphs—that is, images indicating meaning. He notes: "…people should regard hieroglyphs (whether written or pictured) as living things having power in themselves."[38] As such, the images can actively stimulate the wakening process toward expanded awareness and informed decision making. Regardless of your state at the time of the session, contemplating the cards offers an occasion to ponder critical aspects of one's own journey. This takes place from a literally elevated perspective as we look typically down upon the images themselves. Such a healthy detachment can lead to a clarified view of imbalances previously residing within our subterranean realms, so often obscured by multiple layers of confused emotion and misperception. Profound insight can result in

---

36 Hazrat Inayat Khan was born in Baroda, India in 1882 and died in Delhi, India in 1927.
37 Coleman Barks and Inayat Khan, *The Hand of Poetry: Five Mystic Poets of Persia* (New Lebanon, 2012).
38 Crowley (The Master Therion), *The Book of Thoth*. Published originally in 1944 with authorship noted as one of Crowley's mystical names, The Master Therion.

this catalytic process. Author and illustrator of works on witchcraft and folk magic, Gemma Gary notes:

> "Know Thyself" and "All is One" are core tenets of the occultist, and through the work of self-reading as part of one's daily meditations, an on-going invitation and openness to the mirror of the "other" is encouraged and nurtured. The regular act of gazing into it, even via the drawing of a single card, builds through the years a pattern mapping the deeper self and its oneness with that which lies beyond the veil.[39]

Following here are recommendations to consider before looking to the cards for either simple contemplation or divination:

- Do not become overly concerned by the concept-loaded names given to the Major Arcana figures or those of the Minor Arcana's Court cards. Instead, allow the messages of these cards to evolve along with your own understanding through their *visual details*. In this way, you will perceive messages of increasing depth, expanded to include a vocabulary of meaning—quite importantly, those with personal significance—for every card in the pack.

- As will be proposed in the subsequent sections on the Major and Minor Arcanum, each card contains a *range* of messages from "revealed" to "veiled." Keep these fluid since fine shades of meaning can shift easily and dramatically from reading to reading. The encouragement of interpretive flexibility is specifically the reason for the use of "may" or "can" throughout the card-by-card examination to follow.

- The "revealed" messages emphasize light-filled or positive aspects. Generally, they are known or recently experienced aspects or situations, perhaps for the first time. They may also indicate what needs to be embraced as pertains to others, situations, and the self in relation to the focus of the particular imbalance or concern.

---

39 Gemma Gary, correspondence with author, September 2016.

- The "veiled" messages emphasize darker or negative aspects. Generally, these are the ways the "revealed" messages are hidden, overlooked, or misinterpreted, or blocked as relates to others, situations, and the self in relation to the focus of the particular imbalance or concern. They may also indicate unfruitful aspects or situations being released, perhaps for the first time. A fuller discussion of "veiled" messages follows in the subsequent section on reversals in card reading.

- More profound unified messages can be derived when unifying both "revealed" and "veiled" aspects together—by realizing how their seeming separation is illusory. This approach enables one to reach beyond these distinctions to form fully-integrated messages of greater depth.

- The "revealed" and "veiled" messages listed for each card to follow are for suggestion only. Utilize them as building blocks or triggers to be expanded upon through personal contemplation and use.

- Since the cards offer a multitude of interpretative possibilities, do not associate predominately "revealed" or "veiled" messages with any one of them.

- Each card does not indicate messages in isolation from the others in the deck. In some cases, related messages merge between cards, simply expressed from different approaches. Keeping such an open perspective allows the reader to explore and comprehend deeper truths.

- Any single card or grouping of them can offer simultaneous messages. The particular ones perceived or expressed will be determined by your perception and intuitive understanding at the moment of the session, and thus capable of evolving accordingly.

- Utilize all aspects of the imagery in making narrative sense of the cards; this includes, but is not limited to: human and animal figures, inanimate objects (including architectural elements), colors,[40] image composition, and even weather conditions indicated within scenes.

---

40 You are encouraged to refer to a full-color deck when exploring the card descriptions and sample readings contained herein.

Chaos magician and Gnostic explorer, Steve Dee reminds: "Rarely do we rely on cognition alone, rather we anchor experience through the sensual."[41] For the self-reading process, explore every aspect of the imagery for their symbolic and metaphoric values as somehow reflective of *you* first before broadening the interpretative scope to include others and relevant situations.

- View the card's human-like figures as free from age, gender, race, color, creed, nationality, or sexual orientation so they may represent anyone. Even so, be aware that some of these characteristics can be interpreted less literally to stress their symbolic value instead. Again, explore the symbolic and metaphoric value of every figure as reflective of you before broadening the interpretative scope to include others and relevant situations. This concept will be discussed further in the section on the Minor Arcana's Court cards.

- More specifically as for age and gender, interpret these outer characteristics when a figure is visually defined by them as indicative of an inner spectrum of energies. So then, a youth pictured might suggest a behavior, perspective, or situation ranging from one characterized by freshness and enthusiasm to immaturity and egotism. Similarly, instead of an actual woman only, view a female figure as representing a range of classically recognized feminine energies, including nurturing and caretaking. In the same way, a male figure could suggest a range of traditionally attributed masculine energies, including boldness and protectiveness. The key here is that all of these energies as determined by the particular reading can be possessed by you regardless of gender or chronological age.

---

41 Steve Dee, *A Gnostic's Progress: Magic and the Path of Awakening* (Norwich, 2016).

II
Seventy Eight Stations

When I open my mouth I let the gods speak and it is like sparrows singing. When I open my heart I find the way, a gap through the wall of mountains. Through me I allow the world to unfold. I have the magic of earth, wind and flame. Though the future lies shrouded in veils, if I give my will to what I know not, I shall see it all come to pass. No sorrow. No sweat. Knowing the world is as the world should be, I enter the fields of peace.

—Normandi Ellis, *Awakening Osiris: A New Translation of the Egyptian Book of the Dead* [42]

In some mystical traditions, the term station indicates the arrival at an expansion in one's spiritual awareness. This may be the result of a significant experience, from joyful to traumatic, or even via a gently budding insight. While the consequences of such growth may not always guarantee contentment, the undeniable benefit is an existence lived closer to your own truth. Author and spiritual teacher Ram Dass reminds us, "This is the pathless path. Where the journey leads is to the deepest truth in you. It is really just returning to where you were initially before you got lost."[43] Each of the Tarot's seventy eight cards may be viewed as a station along the inner path toward enlightenment. Becoming increasingly aware of their myriad messages through their contemplation and self-reading will aid in this process immeasurably.

The Major Arcana

An Overview

The Major Arcana represents the Fool's journey toward enlightenment—a philosophical quest the goal of which is nothing less than the evolution of the soul. Most of these twenty-one cards, or Trumps including The Fool, feature allegorical figures of deep symbolic power set within highly emblematic scenes. Others show only non-human forms, such as The Wheel of Fortune and The Moon.

The original Italian term for this division of the Tarot was *trionfi* or "trumps." The previously mentioned Italian game *Tarocchi* entails the strategic "triumphing" by cards of greater value. Predating this pastime, medieval Europe gave rise to dramatic presentations designed to teach the masses proper morals and promote religious ideals. In them, characters

---

43 Ram Dass, with Rameshwar Das, *Polishing the Mirror: How to Live from Your Spiritual Heart* (Boulder, 2013).

symbolizing those of a higher nature outdo figures representing baser principles upon an ever-increasing hierarchy of importance. As a possible extension of these widespread productions, processional parades called *trionfi* developed later and were especially popular in Italy. They featured allegorical characters appearing in order of lesser to greater power—mystical and otherwise. Literary examples using similar themes and grading structure survive from the period as well. So then, it is understandable how these popular entertainments may have influenced the Major Arcana's parallel concept and format.[44]

The occult core of such cultural divertissements may be uncovered if we reach further back still. Author and expert in the magical-religious practices of ancient Egypt, Chris Morgan explains:

> Oracles were a defining feature of ancient Egyptian religion. Originating in the beliefs of the folk, their efficacy was recognised by temple authorities, who brought these techniques on-side, and indeed inside. It has long been speculated that European Tarot has

---

[44] Crowley (The Master Therion), *The Book of Thoth*. The radically individualistic and influential Thoth Tarot was created by Aleister Crowley (1875-1947) and the surrealist and mystically-minded artist Lady Frieda Harris (1877-1962). In his guide to the deck, Crowley calls the Trumps the "Houses of Wisdom" or the "Atu of Tahuti"—"Atu" indicating "House" or "Key" and Tahuti being Thoth, the "Egyptian God of Wisdom, magick, Science, also Illusion" (a deity associated with Hermes and Mercury, the Greek and Roman gods respectively). Etymologically, Crowley explains how the French term "atout" derived from Atu is "…short for 'bon atout', meaning 'good for anything', because a Trump will take any card of any suit." Adherents of the Rider-Waite deck, its variants, as well as the Marseilles Tarot, sometime refer to the Major Arcana as "Keys," "Atu," or "Atouts". Learn more about the Thoth Tarot in the following book: Lon Milo DuQuette, *Understanding Aleister Crowley's Thoth Tarot* (San Francisco, 2003).

deep connections to the spiritual quest of the ancient Egyptians. What is certain is that the geomantic and pictorial arrangements seen in tombs reveal the idea of a spiritual journey that influenced the creators of the pictorial Tarot.[45]

The twenty-one Trumps of the Major Arcana can be broken neatly into three distinct sections of seven cards each. While every card offers rumination upon particular aspects of mental, moral, and spiritual growth, the overall themes of each of the three levels address issues of an increasingly mystical nature.[46] This premise dictates the following division among the Trumps:

I   The Magician, The High Priestess, The Empress, The Emperor, The Hierophant, The Lovers, and The Chariot

The first level concerns elemental issues between child and parent; societal pressures, including those associated with organized religion; uniting with a significant other; and maintaining a functional position in the world.

II   Strength, The Hermit, The Wheel of Fortune, Justice, The Hanged Man, Death, and Temperance

The second level involves more complex matters exploring conflicts between one's inner reality and that of the material world, realization of the challenges necessary to overcome such conflicts, and achieving a new level of mastery and unity on a higher plane.

---

45   Chris Morgan, correspondence with author, August 2016.

46   Nevill Drury, *Inner Visions: Explorations in Magical Consciousness* (London, 1994). The author proposes an alternate reverse hierarchy of increasing mystical importance starting with The World and ending with The Fool.

III The Devil, The Tower, The Star, The Moon, The Sun, Judgement, and The World

And the third level relates to the final contests in one's spiritual evolution; the ascent toward a complete synthesis between one's inner and outer worlds; and finally, arriving at journey's end beyond limitations of any kind.

Certainly, familiarity with the individual Major Arcana cards will increase your grasp of these grander concepts. By laying out the cards in three horizontal rows divided according to the levels described helps in discerning the overall design of the above model more fully.

Over time, deeper illumination will reveal how the Fool's adventure unfolds not along a linear pathway, but upon one truly circular in nature. So first, grasp the lessons of the three levels in the more-easily comprehended layout as described above. Then reconfigure these same rows to form a circle, placing The Fool in the center. In this way, each card carries equal significance. From this vantage, imagine the Fool's interaction with each of the Trump figures within their respective scenes. The interrelationships between all of the cards learned from these encounters will surely increase your understanding of the Major Arcana. Such creative contemplation and even further exploring the Fool's voyage through creative imagination or artistic endeavor will provide abundant insight.

For our approach to the self-reading process, the Major Arcana cards represent those powerful motivational forces affecting present behavior and decision-making, thus impacting past and future events. In just as many cases, you may be either aware or unaware of their presence. Consequently, because of the Major Arcana's significance and relative scarcity in the deck—being only twenty-one of the total seventy-eight cards—a session's import rises in direct relationship to the quantity of their appearance in it. Accordingly, choose to conduct readings of particular significance by drawing only from the Trumps.

The upcoming card explanations contain three sections per-card as follows: a description of the particular card's imagery; general comments on its "revealed" or more positive aspects; and finally, some notes concerning the card's "veiled" or darker facets. The interpretative portions of the explanations are a combination of the author's own study and contemplation.[47] As such, use them as building blocks for future expansion through your own discoveries.

For simplicity's sake, the card descriptions and their messages incorporate gender-specific pronouns indicated largely by the images themselves. Certainly, the illustrations were influenced by conventions of the early-20th-century time period during which the Rider-Waite Tarot was designed. However and as noted previously, specifics of age, gender, race, color, creed, nationality, or sexual orientation do not apply in the traditional sense to the figures depicted throughout the Tarot. As will be seen, the reading process will call upon their symbolic and energetic value instead. Let us utilize what might be considered as stereotypes in a creative manner to produce interpretations enriched by an enlightened perspective.

---

47 Suggested by their imagery, several of the card descriptions to follow incorporate non-visual details, such as sound and scent, which are the result of the author's own creative contemplations.

The Major Arcana Cards

0
The Fool

Description

A youthful, androgynous figure is in mid-step high upon a craggy precipice. Bracing, clean-scented breezes ripple the folds of his colorful tunic. A brilliant and warming sun beams down from the cloudless sky. The small sack carried in the classic wanderer style contains everything this traveler needs. A single, white rose is held high in an upraised hand. At the Fool's heels, an equally white dog rears up on its hind legs. Its bark may be a warning to a master or mistress seemingly oblivious to the edge of the nearby precipice.

Revealed Aspects

The traveler depicted here is starting an exciting journey—be it of the standard variety or an internal one of the psyche and soul. Such a voyage can happen at any age. Indeed, this excursion may represent a second attempt at a previously failed venture or one left incomplete or never realized.

Veiled Aspects

As symbolized by the pure rose, the Fool's motivation for this journey may be of the highest order. Even so, the potential hazards to be met, as indicated by the treacherous terrain, should not be underestimated—nor should the dog's caution against recklessness or for ignoring one's instincts. In many myths, a canine companion accompanies certain deities. So perhaps as the Fool starts out, the figure has no awareness of the divinity inherent within the self and manifest world. Comprehension of this essential truth can only be gained through the experience of what is about to unfold.

I
The Magician

Description

A charismatically attractive, robed figure stands beneath a fragrant, flowering arbor. Power from above descends through one skyward-raised hand, while the other pointing downward directs it into being. The ouroboros serpent-belt worn about the magician's waist mirrors the sideways-eight lemniscate symbol above his head, both eternity symbols.  Upon an altar-like table are a wand, cup, sword, and pentacle. The atmosphere of this brightly lit scene is one charged with electric anticipation.

Revealed Aspects

The slight smile lighting the Magician's determined face reveals a confidence borne of genuine ability. The lemniscate symbol and belt indicate a powerful connection with the infinite. Additionally, they connote the self-perpetuation of creativity through its active release. Representative of the four suits of the Minor Arcana, the altar implements of wand, cup, sword, and pentacle declare the Magician's mastery over worlds seen and unseen given their connection to the elements.

Veiled Aspects

A successful idea is nearly worthless without the skill to devise and follow a plan to its realization. What can equally damage the creative process is a lack of self-confidence and the frustration resulting from repeated failure. The unfortunate outcome of such disenchantment can be loss of motivation.

Note: The section on the Minor Arcana will discuss the association between the suits and the elements (see: Pages 85-86).

II
The High Priestess

Description

Within a hushed sanctuary, a seated holy woman stares trance-like between two engraved pillars—one black, the other white. She wears sea-blue robes with a cross upon her breast. The crowned figure holds a scrolled parchment half-hidden within the voluminous folds. A large crescent moon rests at her feet. Filling the air with an undulating drone, water flows just beyond the shroud before which the sacred being sits. A design of split pomegranates and palms embellishes the cloth.

Revealed Aspects

It would be unlikely to imagine a single utterance from the High Priestess other than those of great import, and these only after considerable deliberation. The source of her sphinx-like silence is the possession of a deep and well-guarded wisdom. As signified by the moon, one expression of this night-tide knowledge is via a powerful psychic knowing. She is an unchallenged mistress in this arena, as designated by her Egyptian-style crown. The opposite-colored pillars are a visual representation of the existence of duality in all things, at least on the temporal and even lower spiritual planes. By extension, the same is true of the figure's cross. Comprised of two arms of equal length, this ancient ideogram indicates most notably the meeting of divine (vertical) and earthly (horizontal) forces. The Hermetic concept of duality is first evident clearly in the imagery of The High Priestess trump and then echoed throughout the Tarot in numerous ways. Already mentioned as an implication of Dualism is the notion that aspects of one element may reside in its opponent. This is shown by how the color of the individual alphabetic pillar engravings is opposite to the one upon which it appears. The letters themselves stand for variations of the biblical names Boaz and Joachim, these having female and male connotations respectively. The shroud's symbolically female pomegranate and male palm motif is a further representation of this idea. The emblematic mixing of both gender energies into a single pattern presages advanced levels of transformational understanding to come. Identical to the color of her robes, the nearly concealed waters represent the unfathomable mysteries that, ironically, everyday life unfolds within, but most have no awareness of or access to divining.

Veiled Aspects

Ultimately, knowledge is often best shared if for the good of all, even if only imparted after the accomplishment of some demanding trial. Because of its partial concealment, the word "Torah" marking the scroll is not completely visible. This implies the priestess' potential refusal to divulge her wisdom—here, the parchment being representative of sacred teachings. No good can follow when such deliberate withholding occurs for purely selfish motivations or as a manipulative tool. Conversely, the inappropriate sharing of too much information or the misuse of valuable teachings is equally detrimental. Furthermore, continual reflection without action results in ineffectualness.

III
The Empress

Description

Garbed in a loose-fitting gown adorned with a split pomegranate motif, a regal woman reclines upon cushions within a verdant wood. She wears a crown of stars and raises an orb-capped scepter aloft. A shield bearing the feminine Venus symbol rests against the cushioned throne. A field of wheat rustles in the breeze before her, while a sparkling waterfall splashes into a pool in the distance. She smiles in greeting.

Revealed Aspects

The placid demeanor of the Empress is not one of narcissism. Instead, it displays a respectful self-knowledge of her abundant powers, as designated by the starry crown. She is the eternal maternal—indicated by the Venus symbol and flowing wheat—while giving full reign to the instinctual, as represented by the rushing waterfall. Her voluptuous pose displays an open sexuality and the promise of fruitfulness, as implied by the orb-capped scepter, joining symbolically feminine and masculine forces, and the pomegranate design. The Empress heralds the triumph of the senses over intellect, the joy of living in the moment.

Veiled Aspects

When one applies the creative impulse with discipline in a balanced way, worthwhile productiveness can follow. Hence, bounty without thoughtful direction leads to the wasting of precious resources, whether physical, mental, or spiritual. Alternately, sterility often occurs with the repeated frustration or denial of such dynamic urges.

IV
The Emperor

Description

The authority of this armored figure is undeniable. From beneath a jeweled crown, he stares steadily forward. Ram heads decorate the Emperor's shoulder-plate, as well as the stony throne from which he rules. In one hand, he holds a regal orb; while in the other, he grasps a scepter topped with an ankh, the Egyptian symbol indicating the life force. A thin stream flows steadily beneath an imposing mountain range in the distance.

Revealed Aspects

As masculine consort to the Empress, the subject of this card conversely reigns on intellectual strength unclouded by subjectivity. His concentrated gaze signifies an ability to see past all emotion to analyze objectively any given situation. Even so, the use of brute force in gaining control is an option employed as required. The crown, orb, and scepter are indicators of his unquestioned kingship. His rational planning is critical before he can take effective action. The Emperor is the source of paternal protectiveness on many levels of society—most notably, family, business, and government.

Veiled Aspects

The danger of an unbending mind incapable of considering finer shades of meaning is in its self-defeating limitations. The scene's backdrop of rocky terrain and narrow stream reflect such an austere viewpoint. Evidenced by the ram-head motif, the Emperor's natural aggressiveness may lead to warlike tendencies if left either unchecked or not tempered by acceptance of others' perspectives.

V
The Hierophant

Description

On a dais with a checkerboard design, a pope-like figure sits upon a throne between two pillars. His crown, robes, and scepter are signs of his spiritual authority—as are the two initiates kneeling before him. Within the solemnity of this sacred, echoing setting, he raises a hand in benediction.

Revealed Aspects

The dynamic illustrated by The Hierophant trump is one between a leader and followers—akin to that shared by the Emperor and his minions. Even though this card most evidently refers to such of a religious nature, the message here can easily apply to any organized institution featuring a hierarchy. These may include those of a governmental, business, or social nature. In order to function properly and succeed in their goals, most groups adhere to certain guidelines concerning governance, shared beliefs, and even accepted modes of behavior. Placing the Hierophant in the role of personal conscience internalizes this concept.

Veiled Aspects

Paralleling that of the High Priestess, his feminine counterpart, the Hierophant's negative potential includes abuses by those in authority, particularly in the spiritual realm. The rebel risks exclusion from the master and group in the same way the conforming initiates receive the Hierophant's blessing. However, sometimes discovering individual freedom requires a chess-like game of questioning established conventions, indicated subtly by the dais' checkboard pattern. In accordance with the Dualism concept, the same symbolic color scheme may very well indicate how such a radical view can perceive oppositional aspects residing in most areas of existence.

VI
The Lovers

Description

Within a lush garden stand the nude figures of a man and woman, each before a differing tree. Fiery wings sweeping majestically, an angelic being issues from a cloud. It hovers above the couple offering a blessing beneath a blazing sun. In the far distance between the pair stands a mountain range with a single towering peak.

Revealed Aspects

There is little doubt that this Genesis-inspired tableau is a representation of the Garden of Eden. The Adam and Eve-like figures stand before, respectively, the Tree of Life and the serpent-entwined Tree of Knowledge. Similar to the pillars between which both the High Priestess and the Hierophant hold sway, the twin trees extend the Tarot theme of Hermetic duality. This concept is resolved through understanding, acceptance, and ultimate transcendence beyond it. While this Trump most superficially concerns linking oneself romantically with another, its deeper message can relate to synthesizing seeming opposites of all kinds—even between aspects of the self. Additionally, it is only through advanced insight, as represented by the angel, that one may grasp the human condition as being composed of both matter and spirit, likewise symbolized respectively by the male and female figures.

Veiled Aspects

The lofty mountaintop can indicate the positive outcome of a blessed unity. Nevertheless, disharmony will result when choices are made for self-serving purposes—especially those in which others are involved unwittingly through deception. More simply, losing the love of another is akin to abandonment in a savage wilderness. Furthermore, the male and female figures may represent for many those culturally specific aspects defined as being either masculine or feminine. Conflict can result when these aspects are not reconciled within the individual's personal truth.

VII
The Chariot

Description

A young warrior stands within a chariot drawn by two sphinxes—one black, the other white. What is most curious is how he controls these strange beasts without using reins of any kind. The charioteer's crown and armor attest to his position as protector of a walled city. This metropolis rises in the distance beyond swiftly moving waters.

Revealed Aspects

The arrival of the Chariot signals the Fool's achievement of the first portion of the three-tiered journey toward enlightenment. As such, it represents a significant advancement in maturity realized by assimilating the lessons of the previous Trumps. The charioteer's ability to control the sphinxes without visible restraints symbolizes this newfound development. Here, the beasts denote the potential wildness of his personal needs and desires. Also represented is the figure's further mastery of his dualistic nature, as shown by the headdresses of the subservient mythical creatures, each patterned in an alternating black-and-white design. Therefore, The Chariot signifies a triumph over the self and environment through inner-strength. The idea of victory in all manner of competition can be associated with this card as well.

Veiled Aspects

Self-discipline, even for the best of intentions, can become destructive when balanced perspective or motivation is lost. Moreover, while possibly armored against danger, a walled city that never opens its gates is one equally empty of life's spontaneous wonder. Worthwhile maturation cannot take place if it entails the continual shutting out of others and everyday experience—or most damaging of all, when an individual refuses to confront internal conflicts, the unconscious being represented by the waters. The Chariot also cautions against accomplishment through dishonorable methods.

VIII
Strength

Description

A comely maiden is in the act of grasping the gaping jaws of a fierce-looking lion. The softly growling beast responds with an arched back and extended tongue, its tail between its legs. In addition, just as it does in The Magician trump, the sideways-eight lemniscate symbol appears above the young woman. Rosy garlands adorn her head and waist.

Revealed Aspects

Strength is the first card of the second portion of the Fool's three-tiered journey toward enlightenment described earlier. Starting here, the Trumps will be of a progressively conceptual nature, mirroring and expanding upon those encountered thus far. Therefore, an advanced alternative to the Emperor's outwardly dominating and sometimes intimidating tactics is proposed here. The calm maiden is able to tame the fiercest of creatures into submission via a seemingly gentle approach. More than the infinity symbol above them links the maiden and the Magician. For each possesses an inner mental and spiritual fortitude capable of affecting their external worlds. The floral adornments are further symbols of a power mightier than supremacy through aggression.

Veiled Aspects

In all areas, the Tarot teaches the value in achieving balance. Here, there is an exploration of this in relation to power—both internally and outwardly, between oneself and others. As a savage lion unbound, destruction can follow when the might needed for a particular situation is misdirected. In a converse manner, the absence of power when needed can result in equally self-defeating destruction.

Note: In many decks devised both prior to and after the creation of the Rider-Waite Tarot, the positions of Strength and Justice are inverted—thus making Justice trump VIII and Strength trump XI.

IX
The Hermit

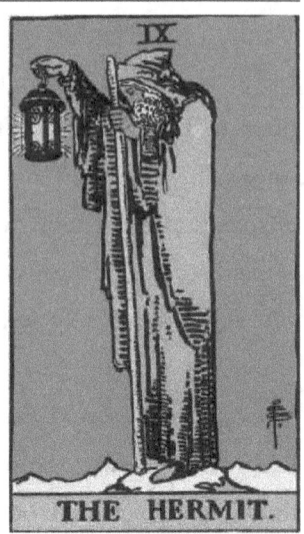

Description

Upon a frigid, snowcapped peak, an ancient figure swathed in a hooded robe raises aloft a glowing lantern. The man's lengthy grey beard, stooped back, and walking stick attest to his great age. He closes his eyes in contemplation. A golden star radiates from within the lamp, lighting an icy wasteland.

Revealed Aspects

The Hermit provides the Fool with an invaluable travelers' tip for the quest—to find the way, look within. Thus, the wizened figure's eyes are closed. Furthermore, while for the same reason he does not require the lantern's light for guidance, his example may illuminate the path for others. The barren landscape can represent a wilderness retreat, far from external distractions, wherein constructive meditation can take place. Do not interpret the Hermit's gender and advanced age literally. In the Tarot's symbolic universe, *anyone* at *any* phase of life can possess the mature wisdom exemplified here.

Veiled Aspects

An excess of isolation—even for the noblest of intentions—can damage a balanced perspective between interior and outer-worlds. In addition, there is an inherent danger in blindly following a superior without an objective questioning of authority. Likewise, The Hermit connects to The Emperor and The Hierophant cards in a common warning against misuse of leadership. Moreover, whether due to feelings of inferiority or deliberate selfishness, the retention of potentially beneficial information links the negative side of the Hermit to that of the High Priestess.

X
The Wheel of Fortune

Description

A fantastical vision dominated by a wheel-like object spins in the heavens to the fluttering of many wings. Surmounted by a sword-wielding, sphinx-like creature, another with a canine head and humanoid body rides its perimeter. Set before the clouds, inhabiting the scene's corners are a winged bull, a winged lion, an eagle, and an angelic being.

Revealed Aspects

The encounters the Fool has experienced thus far have resulted in a profound questioning of one's place in the world and even the very meaning of existence. To come this far, the Fool has had to scrutinize the dualities defining much of conventional society and religion, while relinquishing the ego's confines. Briefly, a visionary realization is imagined here. The by-now familiar double-pillars are nowhere to be found. Instead, an ageless symbol of life's ever-turning nature appears—cyclical, unstoppable, impossible to predict—wherein every ending is a new beginning and vice versa as well. The strange creatures, equally Egyptian as they are Biblical, embody various themes of death and rebirth. More important, perhaps the Fool will notice how the centermost point of the dazzling wheel is the proverbial calm in the changeable storm of human existence.

Veiled Aspects

Truly foolish are those believing themselves wise enough to outsmart the Wheel of Fortune's overseeing sphinx. As hinted at by the mythical creature's sword, unfortunate repercussions will surely follow when there is an obsession with overcoming fate. Facing challenges with honest bravery is best. A levelheaded degree of accepting life's vagaries is essential to progressing on the path to wisdom.

XI
Justice

Description

Between two grey pillars presides a crowned, androgynous figure in judicial robes. Balanced in one hand is a set of scales, while the other holds an upturned sword. A purple veil waves gently between the columns before a bright, sunlit background.

Revealed Aspects

The exact midpoint of the Fool's three-leveled journey, this scene features deceptively simplistic symbolism. Unmistakably, the scale and sword indicate the Trump's themes of impartiality and the karmic, double-edged results of one's actions. Nevertheless, of more interest are the grey columns in comparison to the black and white ones flanking the High Priestess. For unlike those of the earlier card, the messag here is far less obvious. Meticulous examination and acceptance of the vastly complicated grey areas characterizing most situations must happen before the execution of authentic justice. For this very reason, the figure does not wear a blindfold as is traditional with such personifications of the virtue.

Veiled Aspects

More obviously than in any other Trump, illustrated here is the conception of managing duality through a balanced perspective in the traditional sense. Therefore, the consequence of losing such objectivity would be an inability to manage life's complexities—to be unable to perceive the gleaming, sun-like truth lying beyond the purple veil.

Note: In many decks devised both prior to and after the creation of the Rider-Waite Tarot, the positions of Strength and Justice are inverted—thus making Justice trump VIII and Strength trump XI.

XII
The Hanged Man

Description

A figure is suspended head-down, cocoon-like, from two branches forming a T-shape. Green leaves sprout from the wooden limbs. Only a bit of rope binds one of the man's ankles to the top of the cross. A yellow nimbus encircles the figure's head. His eyes are open in serene contemplation. A tremendous silence draws near.

Revealed Aspects

Sometimes taking a radically new perspective is necessary in order to assess a particularly troubling situation or just to view the world in a new way. The figure's inverted position shows this. Furthermore, as signified by the radiant halo, the way to wisdom often happens through just such a shift in perception. However, the process of arriving at a far-reaching goal may require solitary travel—outwardly, inwardly, or both. This might cause others to view the seeker as detached from everyday life. Thus, the figure's open eyes and the crossbeams' flourishing greenery can connote the persistence of activity during an intense period of seeming suspended animation. Likewise, the figure's upside-down, in utero position can indicate a symbolic gestation period of profound transformation. A contradiction between internal and external realms does more than simply illustrate the Tarot's theme of Hermetic duality in a more highly sophisticated manner. This fresh trial to the Fool risks undermining what was already conquered. For unlike the vigorous conscious control of the Emperor and charioteer, the Hanged Man brings about change by seemingly doing nothing more than gently swinging between earth and the heavens. Surely, his acceptance of the dualistic nature of the world and himself without the use of force is one of life's most demanding challenges.

Veiled Aspects

The denial of what is vital to bringing about enlightenment can cause the branches upon which the Hanged Man dangles to become torturously thorn-covered. More often than not, this occurs when the path's genuine challenges and sometime hardships are rejected. The latter include the life-altering changes necessary before the dawning of true self-awareness. Furthermore, this may require a certain degree of inactivity combined with patience—a physical, mental, and spiritual state difficult for many to endure. The T-shaped Tau cross, sometimes associated with a martyr's death upon it, suggests such sacrifices.[48]

---

48 Nigel Aldcroft Jackson and Michael Howard, *The Pillars of Tubal-Cain* (Somerset, 2000). The authors discuss links between this Tarot figure and those central to a variety of cross-cultural myths and religions, including: the biblical Jesus and Judas Iscariot, Odin, and the Persian fallen angel Shemyaza, all associated with hanging in some form.

XIII
Death

Description

Astride a flame-eyed, pale steed, the skeletal figure of Death clad in black armor waves an ebony flag emblazoned with a white rose. Its triumphant approach elicits four different responses from a diverse cross-section of society. A king is struck down, his crown trampled by the horse. A bishop clasps his hands together in prayer. With eyes closed, a maiden falls to her knees and turns away. All the while, a small child, also on bended knees, offers the fearsome victor a floral bouquet and an innocent smile. A distance away beyond the waters, the sun appears between two towers.

Revealed Aspects

The Hanged Man's suspended state has prepared the Fool for Death, although not of the physical kind. Instead, abandoning an egocentric worldview forms the inescapable next step in the process of enlightenment. Regardless of age or status, the evolvement of the individual dictates the nature of one's response to this inevitability. As illustrated by the various figures portrayed, these reactions range widely—from the stricken monarch unprepared for his own mortality; to the clergyman whose sacredness cannot save him; and the woman whose ripe beauty will provide inadequate rescue. However, wisest of all is the guileless child. Greeting the mighty equalizer without fear, the youth celebrates Death's necessary appearance since it signifies a great and inevitable change to come as heralded by the rose banner. It matters not whether the sun is setting or rising amid the scene's dualistic towers, for this journey toward transformation is a cyclical one.

Veiled Aspects

There are many kinds of death other than the strictly physical. The fear associated with each of them forms their common link. Whether the end of a relationship, a period of employment, or long-term residency in a certain place, facing the unknown of what is to follow is often a source of overwhelming stress. This dread is what so often derails the process of reaching one's potential destination. Pain is an unavoidable element of transformation—as well as the acceptance of the dualistic nature of existence as symbolized by the white rose upon the black flag. The denial of this truth is a regretful state of stagnancy. Its appearance here is the final inclusion of the dichotomous, black-and-white color scheme seen prior in the Major Arcana. This is so since from this moment onward, the issues met will be those of a much less obvious and hence more highly advanced and complex nature.

XIV
Temperance

Description

A white-gowned, crimson-winged being rests a bare foot upon a flowering riverbank. Caused by the partial submersion of the other, the waters ripple in a circular pattern. The figure is in the process of pouring the contents of one golden chalice into another identical to it. Tall reeds rustle in the breeze. From this watery source, a pathway stretches upward toward a mountain range. The sun radiates above its peaks.

Revealed Aspects

The tranquil vision presented in Temperance announces the finish of the second level of the Fool's journey. It represents a marked leap from what the accomplishments celebrated in The Chariot at the end of the first level. With complete ease, the angelic being is performing a rather complicated feat—successfully pouring liquid from one cup to another at a seemingly impossible angle, while all the while managing perfect balance upon both earth and river. Water is a universal symbol of the unconscious, as already observed in various degrees in The High Priestess, The Empress, The Emperor, and The Chariot trumps. So then here, that the color of the blue river water and flowing chalice liquid match is not accidental—nor is how the circular formation of the rippling waters mirrors the shape of the sun. For unlike the charioteer's constant struggle for control, the Temperance figure has learned to balance masterfully the unconscious, as demonstrated by the deft pouring, and the material world, as indicated by the earthbound foot. The final leg of the Fool's journey will happen on the road linking the river through to the mountain range beneath the illuminating sun. As shown, this pathway to enlightenment is an upward climb through shadowy terrain, an indication of the next few Trumps and the dark trials to come.

Veiled Aspects

The expert coordination exhibited by the Temperance being is considerable and made possible only through the cumulative teachings of the previous Trumps. Most individuals are not capable of accomplishing more than the impressive skills of the charioteer. Furthermore, for those that do, reaching the journey's next major landmark as demonstrated here requires a sophisticated level of integration. Finally attained, it is one difficult to maintain at best. So jeopardizing this position causes a much deeper imbalance, with results possibly not visible on an immediately discernible level. Instead, the manifested effects might be an inability to keep one's own emotional needs and outward obligations in proportion, or a healthy equilibrium between various familial, social, and romantic relationships. Therefore, as the Fool's adventure evolves further, the risks of catastrophe increase. Nevertheless, so does the worthiness of the potential goal.

XV
The Devil

Description

Comprised of such incongruous parts as bat wings, goat horns, bird talons, and a human torso, an astounding creature holds a burning torch downward while delivering an infernal blessing. Loosely chained to the block upon which the beast perches are nude figures of a man and woman, themselves sporting animal-like horns and stylized tails.

Revealed Aspects

The Devil's downward-burning torch represents an unlimited animalistic passion divorced from higher concerns. Sometimes just such a boundless drive and unhindered perspective are mandatory to reach one's goals.

Veiled Aspects

The Devil's manifestation signals the start of the final portion of the Fool's journey. It is not surprising then that the fearsome creature will prove a formidable sentinel to overcome. The composition of this infernal tableau is in obvious mockery of the positive messages conveyed in The Hierophant and The Lovers trumps. In place of either spiritual patriarch or overseeing angel, the ruling entity here is the embodiment of chaos. So then the careful symmetry of the image is symbolic of an orderly and longstanding mayhem—one wherein the reconciliation of opposites is never achieved. Their easily removable neck chains indicate the minions' willing submission to negative forces. In this midnight kingdom, the pair's bestial features as portrayed here debase the sublime nudity of the Lovers.

XVI
The Tower

Description

This Trump illustrates the precise instant of a cataclysmic event. Lightning strikes an imposing tower either constructed upon or built from the very rock of a perilous mountain peak. A single devastating bolt dislodges the structure's crown-like pinnacle. Two robed figures—one of them crowned—plunge from the flame-engulfed tower to certain death.

Revealed Aspects

The devastation depicted in The Tower is irreparable. It represents a moment of enlightenment once understood will change everything forever. This can take the form of self-awareness or the realization of another's true intentions or motivations. As implied by the lightning bolt, sometimes such transformative insight can occur in a flash. The falling figures and toppled crown warn of the process' potential painfulness and humility.

Veiled Aspects

Undoubtedly, this being perhaps the most violently traumatic image of all the Trumps, the alternative outcome of the scene is ultimately even more ruinous. For in it, the crowned figure—the primary fabricator of mistruths—still reigns supreme in an impregnable tower of lies.

Oftentimes, the key self-deceiver is the Fool when living in denial of what needs to change in order to regain the path.

XVII
The Star

Description

Bathed in starlight, a woman kneels by the edge of a natural pool, possibly the same riverbank in which Temperance's angelic being dips a foot. She is completely nude. From matching pitchers, she pours water both back into the pool and onto the ground. Upon the highest branch of a nearby tree, a single bird trembles its wings. Its welcome song mingles with that of the soothing sound of flowing water.

Revealed Aspects

The utter ruination of The Tower is over. A vista of welcome tranquility follows. With her unabashed nudity in stark contrast to the previous Trump's ferocity, the luminous figure offers curative rejuvenation before the culmination of the journey takes place. Moreover, this nakedness signifies a further shedding of the ego and its defenses. Stripped of all external shields, the maiden's open acceptance of her inner-life has ironically provided formidable protection—a form of psychic armor—against the ego's detrimental barriers to transformation. As a result, the dams of the unconscious dissolve as symbolized by the freely flowing water in a variation on the Temperance figure's studied actions. The surplus fluid spilt upon the earth may betoken how the Fool's inner-resources are now more abundant than ever before.

Veiled Aspects

Often a representative of the soul, the bird sings into the night, free of any restraints as the naked figure is of society's outer trappings. This demonstrates how an excessive need for public approval compromises the type of mystical healing represented here. Without doubt, only the minority take the Fool's enlightening quest. So then, the exceptional travelers on this same path must persist on their way with little encouragement from the general populace.

XVIII
The Moon

Description

Possibly from the very same restorative waters of the previous Trump emerges a crustacean. It appears to be heading for the path last seen in Temperance. Unlike the earlier flowering riverbank, a canine and wolf guard this desolate one. Both are howling at a moon bearing a human profile with closed eyes. The celestial orb is blocking the sun. Two towers flank the forbidding trail leading up through to distant mountains.

Revealed Aspects

Relinquishing the security of a self-centered existence, the Fool's newfound receptivity will allow for the exploration of inner-realms. The successful balancing of his societal self, signified by the domesticated dog, with his instinctual needs, represented by the untamed wolf, all the while accepting his most-hidden aspects, symbolized by the water creature requires considerable courage and the most complex level of integration demanded thus far. However, final reserves of courage are available, if temporarily concealed. For the scene depicted here is not one of eternal night, but of an eclipse. As such a phenomenon, light will shine following the uncommon event's short-lived duration.

Veiled Aspects

Many who reach this, the darkest and possibly most fearful portion of the journey, never continue on to the dualistic towers and mountains beyond. Instead, their goal is lost in shadows of doubt and weakness. The closed eyes of the lunar countenance may imply a mindset dependent upon self-caused rejection and denial of the truth to maintain a desired, if unproductive stasis.

XIX
The Sun

Description

Galloping forth from a sweetly scented, walled garden, a nude child waving a banner rides a white horse. A row of sunflowers borders the wall behind them. A brilliant sun, bearing a human-like countenance and twenty-one radiating rays, lights the scene.

Revealed Aspects

The Fool has survived the darkness. The dreadful eclipse is over. The roundness of the sun itself suggests completion of a circular journey with the implication of yet another cycle to begin again. The child represents rebirth, its outstretched arms signaling openness to a new existence beyond the garden's barricades. So prevalent in the earlier Trumps, here there are no symbols of duality. Everything has been mediated which was once disparate. The sunflowers may represent the four elements and even the suits of the Minor Arcana, thus symbolizing the all-encompassing nature of the Fool's achievement on the terrestrial level—without question, a banner-waving triumph. The open-eyed sun itself stands for spiritual enlightenment and understanding, its glorious light no longer obscured as it had been in the previous Trump. Indeed, the path leading toward The Sun had been lit by celestial bodies of increasing luminosity—The Star followed by The Moon. The number of sunrays equals precisely the quantity of Tarot Trumps. Paradoxically then, this outward sign connotes the comprehensive nature of the inner-illumination arrived at by the Fool at last.

Veiled Aspects

Sometimes, it is easier to hide ourselves in the shadows than to assume a responsible existence demanding clearness of purpose. The very real hardships of daily life, coupled with self-delusion, deflect the light needed as guide to transformation. Regrettably, even though many reach the elevated stage represented by The Sun, it is a difficult position to preserve. Thus for them, the finale of this life-altering expedition is never fully attained.

XX
Judgement

Description

Three nude figures—a man, woman, and child—arise to greet a trumpet-blowing angel from within the tombs that entrapped them just moments before. Similar exultant figures mirror these in the distance. The angel's long-anticipated clarion blast mingles with the sound of waves surrounding the soon-to-be discarded crypts. A banner adorned with a cross depends from the horn.

Revealed Aspects

The association between this Trump and the biblical Last Judgment is undeniable. Even so, it is productive to delve into the card's broader implications. An assessment of the totality of their remarkable journey will take place for the Fool and the scene's expectant figures. Furthermore, it is here that this fearless adventurer will come to understand the crowning lesson to all those preceding it. It is one of ultimate understanding and acceptance. Therefore, like the empty tombs, there is a disposal of previous modes of existence. This takes place once there is acknowledgement of one's own weaknesses and strengths. The time has arrived to leave the interior seas now fully explored to ascend to the quest's final goal.

Veiled Aspects

What a devastating and tragic waste to have journeyed thus far, to have overcome such immense obstacles, and endured self-scrutiny of the most intense kind only to turn back. To embrace the fully integrated self is often the most difficult love of all. Last seen upon the breast of the High Priestess near the start of this adventure, the banner cross represents such a desired state as a symbol of mediating opposites. Terrifying to many is the prospect of a fresh start resulting from such evolvement. Thus instead of beginning anew, any one of the risen figures may ignore the angel's call. This denial results in a return to a tomb-like subsistence in which destructive cycles repeat simply because of their comfortable predictability.

XXI
The World

Description

A resplendent figure appears suspended within a beribboned laurel wreath, partially nude save for an indigo sash about the waist. Each hand holds a wand. Set upon clouds in the four corners of the image are the heads of an eagle, a lion, a bull, and an angelic being. An air of joyful serenity prevails.

Revealed Aspects

A balanced vision of perfection achieved through successfully combining the temporal and the Divine. The Fool's journey is over and any judgment successfully completed. The wands echo the dualistic symbols of pillars and towers seen along the path. However, the holder who controls them both now represents integration. Since the sash obscures the genitalia, there should be no assumption that the figure's gender is female as evidenced by the breasts alone. Indeed, in accordance with the mystical mythology of various cultures, the figure may be hermaphroditic—a visible and ultimate symbol of the reconciliation of opposites. We can reasonably interpret the Fool's androgyny as presaging a transformation both systematic and absolute—from guileless youth, to competent charioteer, to masterful and ambiguously-gendered angelic being, and finally to the sacred and ascendant dual-sexed entity. The pomegranate and palm pattern seen in The High Priestess trump hinted at the potentiality of this metamorphosis early on in the Major Arcana, as did The Lover's couple. The ribbons that wrap about the top and bottom of the laurel wreath, itself a triumphal symbol, recall the lemniscate symbol found above the Magician and Strength's maiden as an indicator of infinity. Matching exactly the corner figures of those appearing in The Wheel of Fortune trump, these four symbols can embody many messages, including: the corners of the earth; the elements of the physical world; and the suits of the Minor Arcana, among others. Excepting the eagle, the significant difference between the other three corner figures and those mirrored on The Wheel of Fortune card is their wingless appearance here. Perhaps this shift from the mythical to the seemingly ordinary is proof of the transformation of the Divine into manifestation. All of these possible interpretations show the journey's comprehensiveness and the celestial enthronement of the metamorphosed wayfarer within their center.

Veiled Aspects

To finish the Fool's epic quest is certainly a pride-worthy accomplishment. However, a terrible downfall would be to assume one's own superiority as a result. Signaled by the circular wreath, the crucial wisdom of the adventure is in comprehending its beginning upon its very completion. For only then will the expert traveler become the novice once more—with the wisdom gained expanding ever vast with the repetition of each new journey.

The Minor Arcana

An Overview

While the Major Arcana tracks the Fool's transformation toward enlightenment, the depictions of the Minor Arcana may seem, at least by initial comparison, quite mundane indeed. However, the student of the symbolically rich Tarot is advised to refrain from forming judgments based upon surface appearances alone. In addition, while certainly grounded in everyday reality, the significance of this portion of the deck is far from inconsequential. Featuring completely illustrated Pips (Ace through Ten), the creators of the Rider-Waite cards understood this fully. To be sure, the majority of most Tarot decks did not include illustrated Pips until this time. Historical evidence confirms how the cards comprising the Minor Arcana predate those of the Major Arcana considerably and are the forerunners of the modern standard playing card deck. However, unlike the Trumps and prior to their connection to the 15th-century Italian Tarot decks, the Minor Arcana grew directly from game-playing cards and related forms originating in Asia and Western Europe.[49]

As for its structure, the Minor Arcana consists typically of fifty-six cards categorized into four suits—Wands, Cups, Swords, and Pentacles.

---

[49] Paul Huson, *Mystical Origins of the Tarot: From Ancient Roots to Modern Usage* (Rochester, 2004). Decks with non-illustrated Pip cards are referred typically to as in the "Marseilles" style. Herein, the Ace through Ten cards feature their representative icons of Batons, Cups, Swords, and Coins. The Rider-Waite replaced the Batons and Coins to Wands and Pentacles respectively for their rich mystical symbolism. Uncommonly featuring fully-illustrated Pips, the late-15th-century Italian Sola-Busca Tarot is believed to have influenced the design of the Rider-Waite deck.

Standard game-playing card suit equivalents are respectively: clubs, hearts, spades, and diamonds. Each of the Tarot suits customarily contains four Court cards (King, Queen, Knight, and Page) and ten numbered Pip cards (Ace through Ten). While this study does not involve correspondences between the Tarot and other systems, one exception is especially beneficial here. A widely accepted and useful association has developed between the suits and the four classic elements: Wands with fire, Cups with water, Swords with air, and Pentacles with earth.[50] According to ancient Greek thought, the elements are distinct components comprising all reality in varying degrees and combinations. Contemporary Devonshire witch Levannah Morgan notes, "…the elements are the substances from which we and the world around us are made, so by working with them we are working with our whole beings."[51]

As discussed earlier, the Hermetic perspective embraced herein views such dualistic energies as matter and spirit as containing portions of its opposite to be accepted, synthesized, and transcended beyond. Similarly, while the imagery of a particular Minor Arcana suit may predominately relate to its associated element, indicators of other suits appear in its cards as well. When this occurs, interpret these neighboring elemental aspects shaped specifically by the suit of the card in question. So then, the appearance of water in the elementally corresponding suit of Cups will take on a different message when seen occasionally in the imagery of the air-based suit of Swords.

Over time, the scope of elemental associations expanded to attribute particular characteristics to each. Aleister Crowley explains: "The word 'element' does not mean a chemical element; it means a set of ideas; it

---

50 Variations do exist between deck types, the suit icons, and their elemental correspondences.
51 Levannah Morgan, *A Witch's Mirror: The Art of Making Magic* (Somerset, 2013).

summarizes certain qualities or properties."[52] In relation to the Minor Arcana, these elemental associations encompass precise personality styles and types of real-life situations ranging from those of brighter to darker hues. Many readers limit the Court cards solely as representing others, while typically not including themselves. In our approach, the Court cards will primarily indicate the self-reader, secondarily others, and so much more.

We can view this section of the Tarot as illustrating different mental, emotional, spiritual, and sometimes energetic traits forming the self-reader's personality or state of being. Their variations are defined by the particular card's suit and rank—the latter being its court position, each of these traditionally possessing certain qualities. Of special pertinence to the Courts is the already-emphasized notion of the Tarot figures' overall freedom from age, gender, race, color, creed, nationality, and sexual orientation. Even so, a mild degree of categorizing in terms of rank and gender can be advantageous in this informed context. Tempered by their suit, following are the main characteristics of the Court cards as defined by rank:

King: an authoritative monarch using aggressive, masculine control, and action; paternal energy

Queen: a knowledgeable leader whose strengths are founded in passivity, feminine control, and nurturing; maternal energy

Knight: an enterprising, but not fully experienced figure acquiring power through risk-taking

Page: a novice eager to learn through life's experiences

---

52 Crowley (The Master Therion), *The Book of Thoth*.

Conventionally, there is an inferred diminishment of sovereignty from King downward to Page according to this hierarchical system. For our purposes, let us perceive a range of meaning of equal worthiness for each of these royals. Once again, regardless of age or gender, we will recognize the Court cards as the self-reader first before considering them indicative of others relevant to the reading. Multiple appearances of Court cards in a reading may represent different, often clashing aspects of the self or those of other individuals concurrently, as well as the development or regression of these aspects across time.

Especially informative are decoding such multiple appearances as personal aspects in conflict within the self. The varied headgear of the Courts are appropriate to their status—from the traditional crowns of the Kings and Queens, to the helmets of the Knights, and the caps worn by most of the Pages. Symbolically, we all wear such adornments in daily life, acting in associated roles simultaneously. So then while an entrepreneurial woman may be the commanding King in the boardroom and then adventurous Knight when seeking out new business ventures, she acts as comforting Queen in tending to her children, yet may remain the perennial child serving as Page when interacting with her parents. Each of us performs similar multipart pageants every day. There are challenges in embodying all of these parts which increase exponentially with a diversity of interpersonal relationships of all kinds.

By further expanding their significance, the Courts can be extremely informative in many fascinating ways. Broaden their scope to connote the mood of a particular situation or even typify an action. A Court card's position in a particular spread and visual relationship with other cards in a multi-card spread will help determine its interpretation as the self or another, personality aspects, moods, or action describers.

The Pip cards (Ace through Ten) depict daily events generalized enough to have universal recognition. Unique among them are the Aces, which form their own subcategory. As determined by suit, each relates to a "realm." This is not to be confused strictly with a physical location only, but instead can serve as a way to describe an especially potent type of situation, place, or focus of concern further defined by its suit. Additionally, the appearance of an Ace signals an offering of the suit's most characteristic, fundamental, and seed-like energy within that realm. The Aces' shared imagery of a disembodied and seemingly Divine hand bearing its suit's icon expresses this idea.

As one method of achieving familiarity with the Pips, first arrange the cards by suit in four horizontal rows from left to right, beginning with the Ace through to Ten. Then attempt to construct linear narratives for each row based primarily on the visual information gleaned from the images themselves. Additionally, apply the same exercise to all of the Pips by reading each row in reverse order from Ten to Ace. Finally, mix all forty cards together to create four rows of ten cards each to be read from left to right and then right to left. It is also constructive to contemplate the Pips by numerical sets; for example, by isolating all four of the Sevens for evaluation. In this way, the common themes between them, as well as how a particular suit shapes each card of a numerical set are more readily understood.

Comparing the abstract grandeur of the Tarot Trumps to the Minor Arcana's outward ordinariness may render the latter as apparently trivial. Nevertheless, such a superficial assessment is deceptive. Indeed, view the scenes of the Minor Arcana as the many ways by which the mystical truths of the Major Arcana are made manifest in the everyday world. Author of numerous books on magick, magicians, and Earth mysteries, Alan Richardson reminds us:

The Minor Arcana is often overlooked, and seen as less important. In fact it is a superb tool which enables you to engineer your own future. In the Quantum Universe, everything that can happen really does happen. Through these apparently mundane but inherently sublime images, you will find a way to set your chosen cards as signposts on whatever path in life you want to take.[53]

---

53   Alan Richardson, correspondence with author, October 2016.

The Minor Arcana Cards

Wands

Above all else, a wand is a tool for action. This can include a commonplace walking stick, a weapon in battle, or an implement in a magical ceremony. In each case, it is the essential instrument required to accomplish a desired task or facilitate change. The wands found in this Tarot suit are actually flowering and therefore living. Their condition as such confirms the Minor Arcana's overall basis in real happenings, and this particular suit's concerns with action and the results of such.

Fire is associated with the suit of Wands. Various forms of action, energy, passion, and sexuality express this element. The spectrum of personality traits and situation characterizers illustrated within this division of the Tarot associated with this element range from: assertiveness to aggressiveness or passivity; courageousness to foolhardiness or cowardice; and erotic passion to licentiousness or sexual timidity. Also implied by the element of fire, these combustible qualities are quickly ignited and just as rapidly extinguished. In magical tradition, the salamander is associated with fire and so will appear more than once in the following cards. The suit's icon is symbolically male, as are the Wands' characteristics typically categorized energetically as masculine. In varying degrees, anyone can possess them. A few examples of actual locales in which events indicative of the suit commonly unfold include, but are not limited to: an active workplace, a sports setting, or an area of physical warfare (domestic or otherwise).

King of Wands

Description

An enthroned King bears a flowering wand and wears a crown with a flame-like design. His cloak and the banner behind him bear the symbol of salamanders devouring their own tails, while a living example of the same rests upon the throne's dais. Leonine symbols adorn the banner, as well as the King himself in the form of a lion-head pendant.

Revealed Aspects

As the highest-ranking male ruler in the suit most associated with action and masculinity of the Minor Arcana, this King is a formidable leader who pursues his goals with relentless energy. The salamander and lion motifs, both symbolic of the suit's element, indicate an intense personality and sexual charisma, while the genuine lizard attests his embodiment of fire itself. He maintains his paternal sovereignty by relying upon instinctual knowledge and an innovative mind. This specific Court figure describes a situation characterized by dynamic happenings demanding cleverness, immediate responsiveness, and boldness.

Veiled Aspects

While the circular form of the salamanders devouring their own tails represents completion and maturity, the crown with its flame-like design is a literal indication of a tendency toward hot-headedness. Sometimes, a negative alteration of this vibrant leader's passionate disposition takes place. When this happens, there is abuse of those aspects securing a dynamic reign for self-serving purposes. Antagonism, arrogance, and licentiousness result. Equally harmful is a leader rendered ineffectual by thoughtless action or a general lack of courageousness. This card also typifies a situation when authority is exploited through anger and flagrant domination, or one in which needed action is foiled through purposeful misdeeds or fear.

Queen of Wands

Description

Upon a throne flanked with carved lions, a Queen sits wearing a blossoming crown. She is brandishing the suit's icon in one hand, and a large sunflower in the other. While flower and lion imagery adorn the throne banner, a very real cat sits ever vigilant at her feet.

Revealed Aspects

As the only female figure of the court, this royal highness embodies the most potent feminine aspects of the suit. Energetic and ardent, her considerable powers of attraction result in unshakable loyalty from others. The rule of this beloved, maternal sovereign is similar to the sun's nurturing warmth, hinted at by the leafy crown and fitting flower. The cat is a domestic distillation of the lion's regal strength, both felines being fire icons linked with Wands. This card can represent a situation marked by achievement through active encouragement or one in which sanctuary is afforded by a capable protector.

Veiled Aspects

The negative attributes associated with cats of all kinds include an enjoyment of predatory games for their own sake and an allusiveness adopted at will. Such are the manipulative ways of this Queen when her authority is corrupted. Disloyal in love, quick-tempered, or vindictive, she has the potential of becoming a dangerous foe when slighted, even if such offenses originate from her own misperceptions. A situational equivalent for this card is one in which control is achieved through taking advantage of those in lesser positions of command through hurtful schemes, outright malice, or even deliberate helplessness.

Knight of Wands

Description

A young knight is astride a rearing horse in a desert. He holds a flowering wand aloft. Red plumes embellish his helmet and armor. Salamanders decorate the tunic he wears over body armor. The lizards' tails nearly meet their mouths.

Revealed Aspects

In age and experience, the Knight has yet to reach the advanced development of the King and Queen. The tunic motif indicates this since the elemental fire creatures do not complete the circular form seen on the King's cloak and throne banner. Nonetheless, this Knight's innate self-confidence and fearless love of adventure are capable of energizing the most hopeless of circumstances. The male symbolism of the budding wand held aloft is undeniable, as is the figure's persuasive sexual appeal. The spirited steed signifies an exciting situation of new possibilities realized and risks taken, perhaps in an exotic setting as shown by the desert landscape.

Veiled Aspects

Since the fire design of the Wands' King's crown is not readily apparent, it suggests a flammable temper under control. Therefore, that the Knight's flame-like plumes and horse's mane appear to be actually burning show an equally explosive disposition, but one less contained. A distorted perception of one's influence or appeal can result in an overbearing demeanor and a self-worth both exaggerated and unwarranted. One can easily imagine the horse symbolizing the Knight himself, throwing its rider before setting off on a dangerously wild rampage. Likewise, this card can stand for a moment or phase of unrestrained abandon when violent anger reigns or there is a disregard for objectivity and morality. An alternate, but similarly unproductive situation occurs when needed action is not forthcoming. As a consequence, indecisiveness or timidity result in missed opportunities for discovery of all kinds.

Page of Wands

Description

In a desert setting, an adolescent Page stands contemplating a much taller, burgeoning wand. A single red feather points from his hat. A pattern of salamanders almost biting their tails decorates the figure's tunic.

Revealed Aspects

This faithful Page performs his tasks as the Knight's attendant with the unlimited energy and youthful zeal indicated by the suit. His eager gaze upward to the flowering wand shows a ready willingness to gain knowledge and expertise through action. Symbolic of the suit's element, the lone hat feather resembles a flame signifying a novice position. This is one soon to be surpassed by practical application of what is learned. Consistent with the Page's role as messenger, the appearance of this Court card can announce a budding situation involving active participation and the potential to experience untried challenges.

Veiled Aspects

Akin in design and message, the incomplete salamander circle design first seen in the Wands' Knight's indicates here the Page's even more profound immaturity in the suit's aspects. A refusal or disinterest in taking the necessary steps to achieve advancement exhibits such childishness. When this happens so early on in his career, the Page's single, fragile flame risks extinguishment. This card may signal a period during which the learning process is intentionally stunted. This may happen due to disobedience, laziness, or needless opposition to a higher authority.

Ace of Wands

Description
Behind a flowering wand held upright, a lone castle rises upon a tall hillside. It overlooks a verdant valley spotted with several flourishing trees.

Revealed Aspects
The foliage of the wand and trees, as well as the valley's lushness, represents a realm characterized by accomplishment through doing. Indeed, the hilltop stronghold is a reality-based example of the potentially rewarding results of this mode. The hand grasps the wand as if to use it for some productive task. This denotes the Ace's offering of the suit's action-oriented energy in its purest form.

Veiled Aspects
The fundamental expression of Ace energy is of an undiluted potency. Accordingly, the vibrant realm of Wands is one noted for an atmosphere of unconcealed assertiveness, liveliness, and even blatant sexuality. Consequently, when this same energy is adulterated or misdirected, widespread domination, ineffectuality, and corruption of all kinds prevail. In these cases, the bestowed wand is either mishandled or brandished as an aggressive weapon.

Two of Wands

Description

From his castellated domain, a figure of obvious high-ranking position looks out to sea. The raised flowering wand held on the turret's edge matches the one bracketed to the wall. He clasps a globe in the other hand and wears a red, crown-like hat.

Revealed Aspects

Seen here is the epitome of the successful entrepreneur. Indeed, he has literally captured the world in his hand. The lofty stronghold and the wand bolted to the tower itself, literally behind him, represent past achievements. As the suit's icon, the latter object specifies how an ability to act effectively when required results in such accomplishments. A future challenge undertaken with the same energetic zest is signified by the wand is his hand.

Veiled Aspects

The quest for something more can result in many victories, and some of these of unanticipated greatness. However, such a mindset can degrade into one of unrelenting obsession and perpetual dissatisfaction. The way the figure looks over the globe, possibly discounting it in seeking unconquered horizons, suggests this potential. Recalling the suit's association with fire, the red cap implies an explosive temper intolerant of those unable to react with the same enthusiasm toward his interests. Alternately, perhaps the appearance of the two wands connotes an inability to reconcile past issues and anxieties with the future leading to a present condition of inactivity. This is an example of the Dualism theme so prevalent throughout the Major Arcana manifested in the everyday world of the Minor Arcana.

Three of Wands

Description

From an elevated vantage and with his back to the viewer, a red-cloaked figure surveys a large body of water stretching out far below. Three budding wands pierce the mound of earth beneath him. He grasps one of the upright-standing posts. In the process, a portion of his cloak has fallen away to reveal the suit of armor worn beneath. Three ships either arrive or depart upon the water's placid surface.

Revealed Aspects

The figure depicted is the embodiment of anticipation. This would apply whether the ships are setting sail on an expedition or returning home from one. For in both cases, the hillside observer's instigations are directly responsible for their voyage. This is reinforced by the equal quantity of vessels and wands, the latter being the action-oriented suit's icon. So then this scene is one in which plans are either made or their outcome manifested.

Veiled Aspects

Success is nearly impossible without some form of liability. Therefore, while the armor represents the single-minded strength required for victory, an inability to modulate this approach can result in insensitive ruthlessness. The cloak of elemental, fiery red suggests a character easily provoked into frustrated annoyance and outright anger. This can be triggered by intolerance of those of a lower rank, even though depended upon to carry out the desired plan. The figure has reached lofty heights shown here symbolically. Even so, he must relinquish any direct involvement in the journey process itself due to the necessary delegation of minor tasks to achieve on an ever-increasing scale of magnitude. Ironically then, the originator of the activity becomes a bystander. Darker still, the crutch-like wand can indicate how disabling insecurities concerning success prevent forward motion.

Four of Wands

Description

Four budding wands topped by a floral garland create an arbor. Through its center can be seen two robed figures bearing flowery tributes, their heads crowned with wreaths. A group congregates to one side, while a bridge stands on the other. In the background, a large, turreted castle overlooks this exuberant tableau.

Revealed Aspects

The scene is dominated by two very different structures—the imposing fortress and the simple arbor. Regardless, the perspective through which they are presented affords them equal solidity and worthiness. Indeed, each is a manifestation or tangible result of the suit's action-based aspects. Even so, the pair of figures link decidedly with the arbor alone as signaled by the floral greenery adorning both. For they, and their followers, are heralding a new order—one that is flourishing, vital, and free from the outmoded strictures represented by the inert stronghold. Conceivably, the bridge indicates a situation of compromise between time-honored and fresh approaches to accomplishing a shared goal.

Veiled Aspects

From a different viewpoint, the two figures have been separated from the group through either their own deliberate actions or by being ostracized wrongly. This dynamic mirrors a similar, destructive connection between the castle and arbor when neither side will cooperate. In such a situation, no comprehension exists of the potential greatness enjoyed by a team. The elemental red color of the turret tops can connote the devastating fury with which the unfairly advantaged establishment can unleash upon a smaller, independent party. However, quite often, only by risking battle with a seemingly mightier opponent can one's convictions be tested and true strength proven.

Five of Wands

Description

Five youths are engaged in combat. Each wields a flowering wand. At least in this phase of it, the battle does not indicate any genuine violence.

Revealed Aspects

The commotion illustrated is a straightforward example of one of the suit's basic themes—progress through action. Additionally specified here is the conflict sometimes required as catalyst to achievement. The image's participants appear equally matched in every way. So then this fact and the absence of brutality between them implies a competition or testing phase within a peer group or between two assemblies brought together for a single purpose. Symbolically, their youthfulness may imply such a contest early on in an association or one concerning a newly initiated project.

Veiled Aspects

Without mutual respect and accepted guidelines, the scene depicted could easily descend into one of chaos and viciousness. Moreover, the explosive nature of the suit's element signifies just how quickly the confrontation can escalate. The uneven number of competitors might suggest an imbalance of power or unfair advantage between two warring factions. Alternately, the visual similarity between the opponents may hint at their being representations of various aspects of an individual at war within the self.

Six of Wands

Description

A figure on horseback moves along in a procession celebrating his recent victory. Similar to the one with which crowns him, a laurel wreath tops the leafy wand he bears. A group of comrades waving similar wands march along at his side. All the while, the white steed looks back at his master admiringly.

Revealed Aspects

While laurel wreaths serve as awards for a variety of reasons, they traditionally connote the attainment of some significant level of success. Within the realm of this suit, this would most readily apply to a triumph requiring swift action. The wand-carrying band shows the team effort involved in the commemorated feat. Even so, the group is recognizing their leader's daring heroism responsible for this win. An alternate interpretation might view the central figure as a clever philanderer receiving the simultaneous adulation of his many, albeit unwitting conquests.

Veiled Aspects

The mounted hero should take heed how, as specified by the suit's element, this glory can be as speedily snuffed out as it caught flame. Furthermore, he ought not presume the attendants' loyalties would remain absolute should his champion status be overturned. For if such an upset came to pass, the relied-upon foundation of his success, represented by the horse, might overthrow him. As for the disloyal lover described above, his amorous balancing act is not only nearly impossible to maintain, but its failure hazardous to all involved.

Seven of Wands

Description

A figure stands near the edge of a precipice. He has taken a defensive stance, wielding a flowering wand in both hands. The upper-portions of six similar wands indicate the position of his attackers on the lower hillside.

Revealed Aspects

With opponents consisting of a single fighter pitted against a half-dozen warriors, this imbalanced skirmish was one quickly ignited as dictated by the card's element. Depicted here is the combat's most decisive moment. Regardless of the outcome, the lone figure is admirably protecting his spot on the hillside. This violent encounter can indicate as well those not waged strictly on a battlefield, but which are just as perilous. Such is the lot of the rebel thinker or minority group member targeted repeatedly by prejudice. The precipice shown conjures the one from which the Fool set out upon to start the quest toward transformation. So perhaps the image here summarizes the resistance of others to the decision of taking on this radical and life-altering journey. At the same time then, it signifies a commitment to a challenge passionate enough to overcome the impossible.

Veiled Aspects

Other than the six wands, not another element of any of the supposed assailants is visible. For perhaps they exist only in the mind of the central figure as faceless threats, unidentifiable but ever-present. In such a state, there is no release of the weapon-like wand as the suit's action-oriented characteristics convert into constant aggressiveness. Conversely, this Pip can illustrate an equally unproductive scenario wherein the figure submits to either real foes or imaginary menace without any attempt at self-preservation. Indeed, such a mindset would consider discarding oneself over the hilltop as preferable to confrontation of any kind.

Eight of Wands

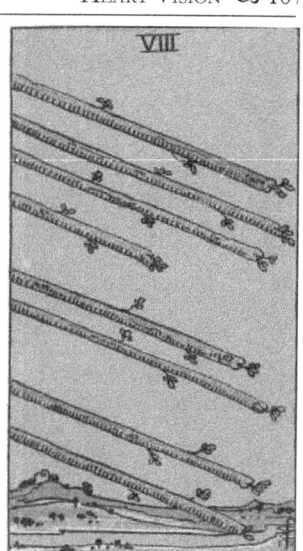

Description

Eight flowering wands descend from the heavens in an aligned formation. Their point of departure remains unseen. Across a body of water, a stone structure stands upon a hillside.

Revealed Aspects

Here is yet another example of the Dualism concept so majestically evident throughout the Trumps brought to earth in the Minor Arcana, and literally so here. The Pip's central imagery of eight budding wands—or perhaps more aptly, four united pairs—reaching their destination only reinforces this quite strongly. In accordance with the suit and element, they symbolize the swift and thorough completion of some action requiring joined forces. In this context, the distant building is representative of the single goal energizing this team effort.

Veiled Aspects

The nearly uniformed configuration of wands may signal an attack from a group with similar aims. The unseen source of the projectiles indicates a lack of awareness of the enemy's identity. Sure to directly influence their target, the wands' downward trajectory defines this outcome as unavoidable and irrevocable. Conversely, this Pip can suggest the indefinite suspension of the desired termination of a situation due to the inactivity, wasteful exploits, or interference by an outside deciding party.

Nine of Wands

Description

A battle-wounded man takes a defensive pose. He stares uneasily in search of the enemy. His weapon of a budding wand matches those forming a fortification behind him. An undulating, mountainous area rises beyond the makeshift barricade.

Revealed Aspects

Other than the suit's icon, the solitary figure is weaponless and without any protective armor. While not a warrior in the typical sense, he is surely a soldier on the battlefield of everyday life. Moreover, his bandage attests to the symbolic wounds he has suffered in this arena. Nevertheless, these temporary setbacks will not cause him to lower his guard. The relevant suit and fiery element describe the figure as one functioning most optimally in energized situations requiring immediate responsiveness. Such a vibrant existence has left him battered, but still able to maintain this post completely on his own.

Veiled Aspects

The figure's dogged glance may contain something more than simple defensiveness. For these troubled eyes seem equally fearful. Sustaining this brand of strenuous control on an endless basis is not only exhausting, but leads inevitably to several unfortunate consequences. For the fighter has shielded himself from the unpredictability of existence signified by the irregular mountain range. He has done so by patrolling a wall of wands built with persistent aggressiveness. As a result, his innate tendency toward belligerence is only enflamed by being in such an unbalanced state at all times. In the end, the paradoxical barricade has afforded him nothing more than isolation, while the unprotected areas between the wands have left him ever vulnerable to life's vagaries. While once a tool of action, his wand has become nothing more than a desperate prop.

Ten of Wands

Description

Using both arms, a figure grasps a large bunch of ten flowering wands. The great effort required by the task forces him to bend forward. A castellated structure stands on the horizon.

Revealed Aspects

Containing the most wands of the suit, this Pip represents expending all available reserves at once. More precisely and in this context, the figure's exertions with the budding icons can stand for the sum of one's action-oriented skills and the courageousness needed to surpass a turning point successfully. Therefore, the far-off stronghold designates the worthwhile outcome of such a struggle. Capable of taking on the backbreaking-challenge shown, the carrier of the wands is a hero appearing swiftly when most needed to conquer a seemingly superhuman feat with impressive ease.

Veiled Aspects

An alternate to confronting a crisis is to either avoid it altogether or become dependent upon another for its resolution. In either case, this scene can describe an individual most affected by the situation in which the same person refuses to become involved directly. Conversely, the encumbered figure may stand for a scapegoat forced to take on an inequitable yoke. Moreover, the corresponding fire element implies the immediate acceptance of such a burden in an emergency setting leaving very little choice. The prospects of eventual breakdown and profound resentment are certainly possible.

Cups

No matter what the form, a cup is a receptacle for what is given or received. It can act as an everyday drinking vessel, a victory trophy, or a chalice in a holy ritual. These examples accentuate the object's prevailing use for purposes of nurturing and as emblematic of a goal or union achieved. The cups seen in the Tarot are sometimes overflowing, empty, or spilt—arguably on purpose or by accident. Whatever their condition, they are always strongly suggestive of the suit's relation to the emotional aspects shaping daily existence and, as such, one's perception of reality.

Water is associated with the suit of Cups. Various forms of emotion, love, intuitive knowing, and maternal attention express this element. The spectrum of personality traits and situation characterizers illustrated within this division of the Tarot associated with this element range from: caring to abusiveness or neglect; maternal to manipulative or selfish; and openly affectionate to emotionally cold or inexpressive. Also implied by the element of water, these qualities are fluid and thus highly changeable in nature. In magical tradition, the fish is associated with water and so will be seen in these cards. The suit's icon is symbolically female, as are the Cups' characteristics typically categorized energetically as feminine. However, as is true of those of the other suits, anyone can possess any of them in varying degrees. A few examples of actual locales in which events indicative of Cups commonly unfold include, but are not limited to: the home of one providing nurturance, a caretaking facility for children or adults, a celebration with family or friends, or a place of romance.

King of Cups

Description

With a crown ringed by a wave design and garbed in blue robes, this King enjoys an unquestionable authority over the seas. Indeed, the dais supporting his throne is floating upon the ocean. Carved lotus flowers adorn the regal chair and mace. While a single fish bursts from the waters, a golden replica of the same hangs from the King's neck. A sailing ship rides the distant waves.

Revealed Aspects

There are many modes to a successful rule. Moreover, while kingly behavior is often associated with action or cerebral-based control, these are not the only ways. Other, equally productive ones exist based on an emotional approach. The suit's icon and element symbolize these, seen here in the crown's wave design, sea-blue robes, water flowers, and both real and ornamental fish. While the Cups' King is no less authoritative than any other Minor Arcana leader, his paternal monarchy is one of nurturance, beneficence, and reciprocal exchange with his dependents. Tossed among the waves, as is the ship, this unsinkable sovereign maintains an equally steady course during the most tumultuous of times. The appearance of this Court card can indicate a secure situation of loving paternal care, received or given, and one in support of inventiveness.

Veiled Aspects

The expression to be "at sea" implies a state of utter confusion, and thus hardly the optimal condition for a King. With the unpredictable nature of the suit's element, the stability of the King's reign upon it can become hazardous without warning, easily capsizing his throne to the depths of the sea. The effects of such an unstable ruler can include petty jealousies, rash decisions, emotional blackmail, and general inconsistencies, all with far-reaching consequences. Furthermore, this card may alert one to a troublesome phase in which supremacy is attained through emotional suffocation or coldness, or a time of frustrated ideas.

Queen of Cups

Description

The summit of the throne from which she rules is in the shape of a gargantuan shell bordered by carved mermaid-like creatures. She concentrates her gaze upon the beauty of an ornate, covered chalice held with both hands. A delicate foot rests upon the multicolored pebbles bordering her dominion of the surrounding sea. A watery pattern embellishes the cloak she wears, affixed by a shell clasp.

Revealed Aspects

In the conventional sense, the Cups' Queen is the most lovingly maternal personage of all the Court cards of this rank. The emotional richness of both the suit and its element combined result in a figure who wields substantial control through emotion and caring. The adornments of shells and undines, these being elemental water spirits, link her to the sea—that is, the realm of the unconscious. Therefore, the intensity of her silent stare displays an ability to ascertain what she needs via intuitive, non-cerebral methods equally effective as more forceful or purely intellectual ones. Even so, while nearly encircled by water, her throne and foot are set steadfastly on land to designate the possession of a realistic mind. The eternal and elusive muse, this monarch appears during a productive period, especially one involving creative endeavors. As symbolized by her highly decorated cup, the scene may typify the motherly act of an affectionate mentor giving or receiving caring guidance.

Veiled Aspects

There is a deliberate lack of differentiation between the swirling waters, the folds of the Queen's gown, and the wavy design of her cloak. This is so since she is completely at one with the suit's element. However, when balance is disturbed, the Queen's finest qualities are deformed. An ever-watchful, motherly gaze becomes one of obsessive and uninvited interference. Intolerance and manipulation through guilt replace infinite patience and selflessness. As symbolized by the covered and closely guarded chalice, the appearance of this Court card may indicate a situation of self-absorption resulting in the denial or refusal of unwanted attention. It may also signal the potential ruination of an artistic project as the result of well-meaning, but uninvited intrusion or lack of imagination.

Knight of Cups

Description

With wings upon his helmet and heels, a Knight rides upon a prancing white steed near a riverbank. The wavy design adorning the horse's reins matches that of its master's surcoat. A fish motif further embellishes the latter. In one hand, the rider holds a large, gold cup that appears to be the focus of his attention.

Revealed Aspects

Purity of emotion can prove to be considerable armor when confronting the challenges of an often-impassive world. With a surcoat and even his horse's reins bearing water emblems, this Knight is the personification of the suit's element and heart-based concerns. Here, the river contrasts with the vast oceans controlled by the Cups' King and Queen. This displays a comparatively narrower ability to manage emotions effectively. Even so, what he does possess is a carefree and life-loving outlook— one perhaps abandoned by the higher-ranking monarchs for securer options with the coming of age and experience. This Knight is the ebullient paramour, as represented by the strutting horse; sensitive friend; or supportive familial peer. The appearance of this card may also signal a period of romantic possibilities or artistic experimentation, and related travel. Moreover, it can mark a time of delving into feelings fearlessly through self-analysis.

Veiled Aspects

Unaware of his limited experience, this fleet-footed Knight never hesitates to act when the heart urges. The symbolic footgear and helmet connote the "flights of fancy" upon which he often finds himself. These futile quests occur when he allows inconsistent emotions to be his only guides, as represented by the upraised, oversize cup. If this takes place, he is at risk of becoming the unfaithful lover, unreliable employee, or perennial victim to his own and others' follies. This Court card can describe repeated patterns of acting on feelings divorced from intellect, leading to potentially hazardous risk-taking behavior. It can also indicate a quickly developing phase of emotional depression.

Page of Cups

Description

A youth in a tulip-patterned tunic and a blue turban stands before the edge of the sea. Fascinated, he contemplates a large goblet held up in one hand. A finned fish returns his look from the cup's interior.

Revealed Aspects

The expected immaturity of this Page does not allow comprehension of the sea of emotions he seems unaware of just behind him. Instead, he looks into the suit's icon—that is, into himself—for guidance. What appears in reply is a manifestation of the element of Cups. The symbolic fish advises self-exploration before the proper reckoning of outside influences can take place. Subordinate to the Knight, this Page is just sensing the amazing diversity of feelings his immediate superior is passionately pursuing. The youth is undergoing an initiation into the world of sensation capable of making the human experience so exhilarating. In some cultures, the tulip is not only a symbol of love, but also more specifically, the declaration of that emotion. So then, this Court card may herald the initiation of an amorous liaison, or simply a situation of giving and receiving new sentiments and sensations for the first time.

Veiled Aspects

Unlike the well-defined contours of crown or helmet, the top of the Page's undulating turban appears to be a splash of water. Indeed, its sea-blue color coordinates with the wearer's tunic and connects them both to the ocean of unconscious experience. The indistinct shape of the hat represents a fragile developmental state as expressed through the figure's rank and element. Difficulties surface by disrupting emotional growth this early on. The consequences can be an individual unable to articulate their own basic emotional needs. This can lead to a failure to integrate these with those dictated by society of a more complex nature. So then the appearance of this card can indicate a situation halting or ceasing emotional maturation altogether due to conflicted or misunderstood feelings. These same reasons can prematurely derail an artistic project, preventing a needed muse from appearing early on in the creative process.

Ace of Cups

Description
Upon an open palm rests a golden chalice emblazoned with a inverted letter "M". Five streams issue from the vessel's interior to spill into the large body of water below. A white dove bearing the sacred host hovers above the cup.

Revealed Aspects
This image is one largely comprised of Christian iconography. Uncommon among these symbols is the upside-down letter, most probably signifying the Virgin Mary. Its recumbent position can suggest a realm abundant with the most giving aspects of the suit. They are largely universal regardless of religious denomination and include maternal nurturance, creativity, and generosity through sacrifice. The position of the palm-up hand supporting the cup is one clearly of selfless benevolence representing the suit's love-centered attributes.

Veiled Aspects
Conceivably, the most disturbing realm of all the Aces may very well be one in which a lack of caring, or even violence, impairs the Cups' abundant energy. Such a dark sphere of existence occurs when a mediation of opposites cannot be reconciled. With its intersecting arms of equal lengths, the host's cross recalls the similar icon seen in both The High Priestess and Judgement trumps—here, used again as a duality symbol. The five gushing rivulets could stand for the Tarot as a whole, consisting of the Major Arcana combined with the four suits of the Minor Arcana. So refusing this Ace's offering—a desecration of the altar bread shown—can result in an all-encompassing sterility on both spiritual and temporal levels.

Two of Cups

Description

Each crowned with a wreath, a couple share a moment of union. A fabulous vision rises between their golden cups. In the distance, a cottage is nestled amidst rolling hills.

Revealed Aspects

The intensity of the connection between these two figures is palpable. This is the rarest of occurrences in which complete integration takes place. Moreover, it is through such a catalytic bond something greater than its components is produced. The fantastical image seemingly manifested from the pair's act of alliance illustrates this concept. It is an amalgamated symbol comprised of Egyptian and Roman icons—most relevant among their meanings is that of transformation through the joining of opposites. The scene here can be viewed as a more terrestrial version of The Lovers' mystical couple or even the unified figure of The World. Alternately, here the two figures can represent divergent aspects of the same individual. Remarkable personal advancement on many levels can happen when these merge successfully. So then, the scene's dualistic dynamic is yet another instance of the potentially marvelous outcome of the Tarot journey through the reconciliation of opposites.

Veiled Aspects

As an interpersonal goal, the small homestead may suggest a mutually inhabited domicile or a symbol of bringing together two lives for a single purpose. Considering the figures' far proximity from the cottage, an arduous trek would be required to reach it. However, this challenge may not happen when the commitment and self-sacrifice often necessary for a beneficial relationship are absent. Furthermore, the house's isolated situation can connote a union unchecked by reality, and therefore one possibly destructive to its residents—either individually or as a unit. As implied by the suit's sensual aspects, this coupling may have begun as a romance or sexual liaison, or situation of initial nurturance. Regardless, the wreath crowns connote how the conjunction may be one recognized officially in a marriage ceremony or business partnership. Recalling The Lovers once more, this Pip card can signal as well a situation of dualistic inner-turmoil caused when an individual cannot mediate conflicting issues.

Three of Cups

Description

A trio of maidens raises golden goblets skyward within a flourishing field. Their interlocking positions suggest this movement to be part of a dance or even a ritual. A flowering wreath crowns each of them. One of the maidens grasps a bunch of grapes.

Revealed Aspects

As a harvest celebration, the figures are enjoying the literal fruits of their efforts. This reward would not have been possible without the necessary dedication, compromise, and shared vision vital to any collective endeavor. The group's matching wreaths betoken their common aspirations. A less obvious reading of the scene might interpret the maidens as being diverse facets of the self. Whether representing an actual group or an individual, the trio's stylized movement signifies the fluid functioning of divergent elements. Within such an abundant setting, this image assures of the potential riches—in every sense, including the mystical—available with the surpassing of duality.

Veiled Aspects

In the nurturing context of the suit and expansive nature of the relevant element, this Pip can relate to joint ventures involving the loving assistance and maternal care of others. It may also illustrate a classic love triangle or three portions of an individual's emotional life. Most harmful to a thriving version of these dynamics is an imbalance of some kind. That only one of the figures holds the grapes may indicate such an inequality. Herein, a single person within a unit or aspect of the self is given, demands, or takes inordinate attention away from the others.

Since the suit of Cups encompasses emotional misperception, such preferential treatment may be a delusion only stemming from jealousy or distrust within a group or conflicted emotional needs within the self, either way resulting dangerously in fragmentation and possible disintegration.

Four of Cups

Description

With eyes downcast and both arms and legs crossed, a figure sits upon a hillside beneath a tree. Three upstanding cups rest upon the ground before him. A disembodied hand issuing from a small cloud presents an airborne fourth.

Revealed Aspects

Enticements are always a danger when one attempts to maintain focus on a particular goal. This is especially so when those distractions are of an all-pervasive emotional nature, as implied by the suit's fluid element. In this context, the scene's subject is exhibiting strength of will capable of resisting such temptation. Conceivably then, the figure has adopted a meditative pose for a journey inward. There is a summoning of spiritual resources through this contemplation as signified by the visionary cup. The tableau's tree easily recalls the Bodhi Tree beneath which Gautama Buddha reached enlightenment.

Veiled Aspects

Emotional distortions are common in the realm of this suit. Here, the figure's intentional position displays such a possibility in one effectively blocking reality. Moreover, this has been successful enough to prevent comprehension of the extraordinary as well, indicated by the apparently unseen airborne cup. This same manifestation resembles the bestowment of fundamental energies common to all of the Minor Arcana's Aces. Within this particular suit, the numinously delivered vessel may betoken an unanticipated emotional force ultimately capable of stabilizing the recipient's imbalanced perspective. Sadly, the gift is unnoticed or rejected due to a state of isolated disillusionment. Furthermore, the youthfulness of the figure does not necessarily designate any definite age-range. It may represent instead a period of disenchantment and cynicism occurring early on in a situation under scrutiny.

Five of Cups

Description

A black-cloaked figure stands along a riverbank with bent head. Before it are three overturned cups, their contents spilt upon the ground. Two other cups remain standing behind. A bridge over the waters leads to a hillside fortress.

Revealed Aspects

Completely enveloped in the blackest of sorrow, no amount of mourning can replace what was lost from the overturned goblets. This dismal state is so consuming as to prevent awareness of the two cups still standing. Represented by the flowing river, the Pip's suit and its associated element indicate a grief connected with familial, romantic, or even chaste love. The bridge can signify the requisite process of overcoming this anguish before emotional stability can be reestablished, the latter connoted by the tower. By this interpretation, the pair of upright cups signifies the hope remaining after tragedy strikes.

Veiled Aspects

Sometimes the victim of an emotional catastrophe is more intimately connected with the continuance of a misfortune than is outwardly apparent. As illustrated here, the figure has deliberately bent its head to view the world only through the cloak's gloom. In a similar way, some individuals attract and foster calamity as a means of becoming self-important or obtaining sympathy from others. Alas, what will often be received instead after a time is disdain and avoidance. Alternately, the solitary figure may be truly isolated in misery without support of any kind. By this meaning, the very hope the two cups offer results in their rejection. This is so since faith in their promise is to risk further and potentially greater disappointment. In the end, the bridge serves as an escape route to a lonely tower of self-perpetuating gloom.

Six of Cups

Description

Within a village square, an older child presents a younger one with a flower-filled cup. There is a display of other vessels likewise adorned. The figures are unobserved by a spear-carrying sentinel walking away from them.

Revealed Aspects

Shown here is a moment of selfless giving. The suit itself and appearance of the children determine this as a manifestation of some form of nurturance or love of the purest nature. What makes the gift especially meaningful is its bestowal from a deeply emotional level without concern for society's restrictions as represented by the sentinel. For many, an unavoidable part of reaching maturity is an over-concern with others' opinions. Unfortunately, these are often censorious to spontaneous expressions from the heart. This image illustrates a childlike gesture free of any such trepidation or obligatory reciprocity.

Veiled Aspects

That the benefactor is just slightly older than the girl may signal the latter's naïve acceptance of advice from an inexperienced source. Conceivably then, the act between the pair takes on a clandestine tone if performed deliberately without the sentinel's awareness. If this is so, either one or both of the central figures may be perpetrating a questionable exchange under an innocent guise. Keeping in mind the suit's characteristics, another interpretation may perceive the girl's youthful age as symbolically indicating an immaturity forever demanding of others' emotions. The negative aspects of the relevant element would prove this an exhausting experience for those providing such constant support.

The assembly line of cups represents this unquenchable need. For they require constant replenishment without any true appreciation from the recipient.

Seven of Cups

Description

Turned away from the viewer, a figure observes a fantastical vision emanating from a cloud. It appears in the form of seven cups. A different emblematic form rises from each golden vessel.

Revealed Aspects

A celestial head, a shrouded being, an uncoiling snake, a castle built upon a mountain peak, a collection of glittering jewels, a laurel wreath, and a hissing dragon preparing to pounce. The exact meanings of these symbols are imprecise, debatable, and varied at best. Of more importance are their overall thematic value spanning from the fearful to the desirable. As signaled by the emotion-driven suit, the Pip provides a depiction of the internal complexities involved in any decision-making process. A deeper reading of the cups' contents can define them further as possessing either divine or earthly aspects. The most informed determinations are those made when one possesses the ability to perceive accurately the potential of either or both inherent in a particular choice.

Veiled Aspects

An abundance of awe-inspiring options can be a paradoxical hindrance when a needed determination is pending. This is especially so when the suit's elemental trait of indecisiveness is just as amply evident. Depending upon the uncertainty of the individual and specific situation at hand, the seven icons can betoken a selection of available choices or separate aspects of a single one. A closer look at the upper-portion of the cup holding the victory symbol of the laurel wreath reveals a death's-head. In addition to its popular significance for mortality, a skull can stand for the truth beneath outer-appearances as well. So then the spectator's bedazzlement renders him incapable of discerning fully the ramifications inherent in every choice, perhaps leading to disastrous consequences.

Eight of Cups

Description

With the aid of a walking stick, a cloaked figure begins an upward climb upon uneven terrain near water. What remains behind is a series of golden cups, some stacked upon others. As the result of a possible lunar eclipse, shadows darken the scene lit by a moon with a humanoid countenance.

Revealed Aspects

The multiple cups suggest a ready supply of the suit's most positive characteristics—love in many forms, nurturance, and emotional release. Hence, the figure's abandonment of them and the eclipse itself heralds an expeditionary phase defined by a timeframe or other parameters during which these aspects are set aside to explore different or new concerns. Then perhaps the moon face becomes that of the journeyer viewing and reassessing the self from an objective distance. It is not coincidental how the stick-carrying figure depicted is reminiscent of The Hermit since both share this wise trait essential to the transformative quest.

Veiled Aspects

When emotion alone becomes a guiding force, as suggested by the cups' prominence in the image, a hindrance occurs on the first step toward enlightenment. For many, the seductive lure of losing oneself in an emotional whirlpool is preferable to the undeniably painful separation from what is comfortably familiar. This is true even if these customary modes of existence result only in stagnancy. The lunar influence on the suit's element reflects such a cyclical return to unconstructive complacency. So then, while a golden cup often serves as a winning prize, the situation described thusly promises nothing but perennial loss and failure.

Nine of Cups

Description
With a wide smile lighting his ruddy countenance, a turbaned figure sits on a bench. The man's arms cross his chest. Behind him upon a tall platform rest nine neatly arranged, golden cups.

Revealed Aspects
The reverential position of the cups on the altar-like table implies the elevated regard their owner holds for their contents. While this would include the love-based and nurturing aspects designated by the suit, the relevant element signifies a liberal sharing of their abundance by the possessor. In this way, the scene can illustrate a situation wherein a benefactor provides needed assets. More specifically, these are not of a quantifiable type since support and guidance generated by jovial kindness are beyond measure.

Veiled Aspects
The wealth of cups and even the figure's corpulence are emblematic of a hording of the suit's finer attributes. In addition, the man's crossed arms block his heart symbolically. This protectiveness averts the formation of emotional connection with the outside world. For any such giving or receiving in this realm might possibly cause the draining of what he has stockpiled. Nevertheless, these cups are for sharing. Instead, a solitary celebrant in an excessive banquet for one raises them. In this way, this scene can represent an overly guarded individual attempting to control an emotionally charged entanglement by withholding appropriate expressions of feeling.

Ten of Cups

Description

A family stands a distance away from their countryside abode. A river flows from the direction of the house. While the two adults greet a rainbow of golden cups spread out across the sky with open arms, a pair of children frolics together with clasped hands.

Revealed Aspects

With its similar bowed shape, the rainbow is a form of celestial bridge. Therefore, those crossing this particular one will receive everything promised by what the suit's icons adorning it connote. Here, the traditional family unit pictured expands to include any group joined together through mutual love, admiration, or caring. The multi-colored bands comprising the single rainbow signifies the potential diversity of its members united beneath these emotional aspects. The dancing children are an expression of the boundless joy waiting in the homestead where fulfillment is abundant.

Veiled Aspects

The manifestation of a rainbow is a fleeting moment of natural beauty—perhaps even one hinting at divine happiness. Sometimes, the unexpected appearance and quick termination of such a blissful phase brings more lasting heartache than joy in its brevity. Alternately and in a darker light, the perhaps too sugary perfection of the tableau as a whole may suggest something deeply problematic and concealed from casual view. This reading views the image as the portrait of a family linked by a secret burden. Regardless of its specifics, the group maintains a calculated façade to hide this painful reality. The two sets of joined figures and the house itself represent this contained effort. However, the tendency of the suit's element to overflow when disrupted can indicate a coming inability for the group to withhold the truth forever. On an individualistic level, the Pip may signify a basic incongruity between one's inner-turmoil and outward cheerfulness.

Swords

Rarely does one wield a sword for frivolous matters. As a battle weapon, a decorative emblem of strength, or a ceremonial blade in a sacred rite, the outcomes of its uses are usually decisive. Accentuating this fact is both its sharpness and universal recognition as a power icon. In addition, its double edges illustrate the inherent twofold nature of a required choice. Perhaps this is why the scenarios pictured in this suit are the most challenging of all four. Indeed, they do include disturbing visions of treachery and symbolic bodily harm—as well as ones of a less dramatic, but still anxiety-provoking nature. They are strongly suggestive of the suit's relation to the intellect, as well as the difficult decision-making processes irreparably determining one's existence.

Air is associated with the suit of Swords. Various forms of intellectual knowledge, communication, asceticism, and impartial decision-making express this element. The spectrum of personality traits and situation characterizers illustrated within this division of the Tarot associated with this element range from: intellectual brilliance to partial understanding or ignorance; unbiased judgment to self-interest or prejudice; and clarity of choice to confusion or anguish. Also implied by the element of air, these intangible qualities are sometimes not readily observable in others, or even in the self. In magical tradition, the birds and other winged creatures are associated with air and so will appear sometimes in this suit. Although capable of being possessed by anyone in varying degrees, characteristics associated with the Swords are usually categorized energetically as masculine, this indicated by the obvious male symbolism of the suit's icon. A few examples of actual locales in which events indicative of Swords commonly unfold include, but are not limited to: a place of higher learning; a courtroom; a setting of mental anguish, imprisonment, or grief; the boardroom; or a retreat where mental reflection can take place.

King of Swords

Description

A monarch sits upon a throne bearing a carved relief of butterflies and winged beings. With a crown adorned by a cherub and holding an upward-pointing sword, he looks directly forward from the center of the scene. Two birds sail through the distant, cloud-filled sky.

Revealed Aspects

Of all four Minor Arcana Kings, he is the only to make direct eye contact with the viewer. This provides a defining characteristic of the entire suit—the frequently uncomfortable analysis of the self, others, and life situations in an effort to uncover truth. Thus as sovereign of the Swords, his perspective is the most objective. The sword's distinct double edges depict his ability not only to scrutinize both sides of an argument precisely, but also to articulate the results in an accurate manner. Far above any obscuring emotional entanglements, the soaring birds' lucid viewpoint illustrates this ability. The butterflies, winged beings, and cherub are all creatures of the air, thus proclaiming this King as master of the suit's element. Situations indicative of this card are those requiring the giving or receiving of honest and candid opinions, regardless of severity, for ultimately beneficial purposes.

Veiled Aspects

The King's throne rests upon a hilltop in such a way as to appear set among and, more significantly, even above the clouds beyond. This depicts the potential of an impartial intellect elevated so high as to result in disconnection from any reality-based matters. When this occurs, there is the added menace of a sadistic mind lording over others through mental abusiveness and malevolent trickery. Conversely, the rule of a maladaptive King in this suit includes acts of prejudice and favoritism, with the consequential inability to make fair decisions. The appearance of this Court card can describe unjust and cruel mental conditions either experienced or meted out by a paternal figure. Furthermore, it can specify an extremely frustrating phase when there is a delay or intentional denial of a desired decision from a superior.

Queen of Swords

Description

Set against a windswept background, a Queen sits in profile upon a throne with carvings of a cherub and butterflies, the latter comprising her crown as well. In one hand, she points a sword heavenward. From the wrist of the other raised in a regal gesture, the severed end of a rope bracelet hangs. The motif of clouds upon the cloak enfolding her mimics those filling the sky pierced by a single bird in flight.

Revealed Aspects

The element of air in itself is nearly impossible to illustrate graphically. Although as depicted in this tableau, its potent effects are visible. The swaying trees, rolling clouds, and even the flight of the bird are each influenced by or dependent on the suit's elusive element. In the same way, the reasons for the exacting decisions of this monarch are not always obvious at first. However, rarely is her wisdom proven unsound with the passage of time. The sword and severed rope bracelet symbolize her capacity to cut away self-delusion and falsehoods in the painful process of resolving troublesome quandaries. All the same, this maternal sage demands nothing less of others than the intelligence and sincerity she expects from herself. While admired unconditionally, her methods are sometimes difficult for others to comprehend. For finally, it is understood how the truth she seeks in everything provides the freedom that follows directly from it. Similarly, this card implies a situation of judgment for someone's betterment or one when a dispassionate stance is essential to sorting out a problematic issue.

Veiled Aspects

Holding sway from her throne in the clouds, the potential exists for this Queen to become intolerant of others perceived as unequal to her high standards in every way. The figure's position of full-length profile can imply a one-sided nature. If so, the resultant deceptiveness, hypocrisy, and malevolence would prevent her from governing with any sense of genuine honesty. The appearance of this Court card can demonstrate an unfortunate state when scheming or treachery by someone in a dominant, perhaps maternal position hinders advancement. Likewise, it can point to ill-treatment through spiteful behavior toward those who should receive support instead.

Knight of Swords

Description

A sword-wielding Knight races uphill, his helmet's feathery plume caught in the breeze swaying the far-off trees and shifting the clouds. Butterflies and birds embellish the breast collar of his galloping horse. A small emblem of a heart adorns the mount's harness.

Revealed Aspects

The Swords' Knight is the personification of the active aspects of the suit's element, as illustrated by the breast collar's butterfly and bird motif. Possessing the unbounded energy and daring of his rank, he can provide remarkable ideas with little preparation, as shown by the upraised sword. He conveys these effortlessly in accordance with the suit's flair for eloquence. This Court card can represent those moments of crisis in which rapid thinking and valiant decision-making skills are required before fear deters them. It can also imply a sudden journey undertaken at a moment's notice.

Veiled Aspects

The figure here is hurrying along an arduous uphill track. Nevertheless, it is one he chooses repeatedly and of his own volition. Along it, the Knight's hasty response to every challenge leads frequently to error and wastefully redoubled efforts. So then, the helmet feather may symbolize such a quick, but rash-thinking mind. The diminutive size of the heart emblem connotes this fickle Knight's tendency for whirlwind infatuations, instead of an expansive, long-term love affair. The appearance of this card can describe a regretful situation when a modicum of forethought would have been enough to prevent it. Additionally, it can typify repeated cycles of ineffectiveness due to a lack of planning or commitment.

Page of Swords

Description

Poised upon a hillside, a Page raises his sword with both hands as if prepared for battle. The winds hurrying the clouds across the skies blow his longish hair upwards. A small flock of birds circles overhead.

Revealed Aspects

Armed with the suit's icon, the Page is keen to aid his leader with bright ideas from a childlike mind unimpeded by pessimism. With youthful ease, he applies such innovative thought equally to topics ranging from the insignificant to more lofty ones, the latter suggested by his hillside position. In addition, as implied by the invigorating breeze stirring the Page's hair and clouds, his is the sought after gust of mental fervor needed when ideas are lagging. This card may proclaim the start of an invigorating phase of academic discovery. Furthermore, it can signal a previously unthought-of perspective on a past issue. Additionally, it can show regained interest in a former intellectual pursuit.

Veiled Aspects

The tiny group of birds riding the winds appears to be forming a circular pattern. This symbolizes the Page's potential entrapment in a round of pointless and impractical ideas. When this occurs, he can become the inappropriate underling who attempts to insert his opinions in matters reserved for those of higher rank. Overall, it can imply the premature narrowing of one's mind or the limiting of perspective, especially by outdated, prejudicial, or juvenile notions. The appearance of this Court card may indicate the beginning of what proves to be a persistent situation of self-questioning and insecurity.

Ace of Swords

Description
The tip of an upright sword pierces a golden crown adorned with swags of evergreen. The backdrop is one of an austere mountain range.

Revealed Aspects
The realm of this Ace is a place of unadorned honesty absent of any misleading shadows. The pristine mountains indicate this in conjunction with the suit. The crown, a symbol of material existence, penetrated by the sword, one of the Tarot's main icons for objectivity, illustrates this interpretation most dramatically. The hand position designates the bestowment of this Ace's energy as one best taken up and implemented to clarify emotionally unbalanced situations and rectify unjust conditions.

Veiled Aspects
As an eternity emblem, the evergreen swags signify the perpetual energy of unbiased truth available in this realm. Nevertheless, the same can become a state of deception and prejudicial discrimination once adulterated. Sometimes, a temporary success results from the refusal or wielding of this Ace's essence of integrity for self-serving ends. Frequently though, the eventual delusion and dishonesty to follow will impart unpleasant circumstances as enduring as the evergreen.

Two of Swords

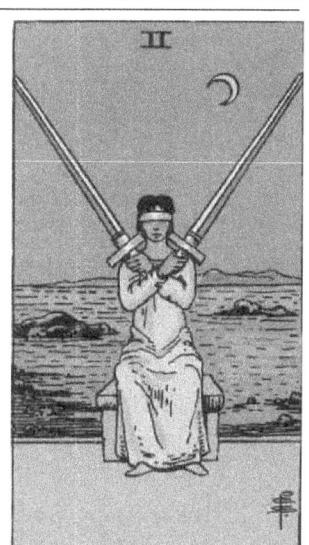

Description

A blindfolded figure sits by the edge of a large body of water with crossed arms over its chest. It holds upward two large, double-edged swords. The top portions of a pair of stony formations break the water's surface. A waxing moon lights the dimly lit, nighttime scene.

Revealed Aspects

A facet of the suit's cerebral domain, this Pip explores the problems inherent in a decision-making situation. The figure's crossed arms parallel or even multiply the two swords, which are double-edged. All of these imply the dualistic nature of most choices in which any one outcome may contain both positive and negative aspects. The figure's blindfold signifies an inability or refusal to face an impending decision. The result is a tableau in which debilitating stagnancy hides behind an appearance of balance and tranquility. However sometimes, there is value found in adopting such a stance as a means of refraining from committing to a verdict until a well-informed judgment can be better determined.

Veiled Aspects

With water as a frequent Tarot symbol for the unconscious, its prominence here indicates just how profoundly the decision process is distressing the figure. Specifically shaped by this suit, such upset may be taking place on an intellectual and thus anxiety-producing level. The lunar phase of a waxing moon occurs with the expansive movement from a new moon to a full one. Symbolically then, this signals how the situation depicted here is quickly reaching a crisis level—one which can no longer be ignored. Indeed, the lack of symmetry between the two rock formations represents an imbalance or very real breaking point in the figure's control of the previously maintained state of affairs.

Three of Swords

Description

Three arrows pierce and affix a blood-red heart to the heavens. The inserted blades create an orderly formation. A steady rain falls from the surrounding clouds.

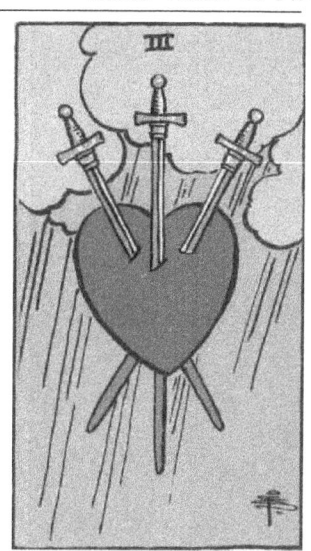

Revealed Aspects

With its combined universal symbols of heart and swords, the splendor of this image elevates it to the level of classic religious iconography. Fundamentally, the emblem suggests an injury and its consequential pain. Moreover, the suit's elemental association with the intellect specifies the effected site to be the mental sphere. The symbol's precisely balanced design suggests an agony not only accepted, but one also converted by the sufferer into a source of positive strength. As such, it becomes the noble heart of the martyr from whose torment the less fortunate or unaware benefit. The cleansing rainstorm connotes a momentary respite from such continuing misery. Alternatively, as no shower lasts forever, it may insinuate the hurt's eventual cessation.

Veiled Aspects

Regardless if the heart wound is self-inflicted or made by another, the symmetry of the swords can imply a deliberateness of intent. In either case, it may represent an unresolved grudge or a calculated act of vindictiveness. Inherent in this suit is the ability to function on a purely cerebral level, divorced from emotional concerns. Therefore, when a misdeed is committed with this kind of detached approach, the perpetrator and the recipient both become victims, linked through mutual negativity. This applies as well to the individual involved in self-destructive behaviors. Additionally, the swords can symbolize the past, present, and future. In this context, the person exists while caught in a perpetual state of melancholic anguish attached to all three, paralyzed as if pinned to the rain-filled skies.

Four of Swords

Description

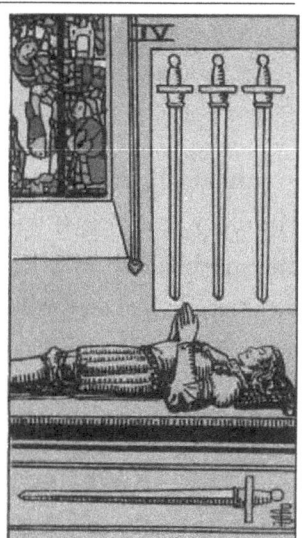

A tomb dominates a chapel. The lid of which is adorned by the sculpture of a recumbent figure in armor, its hands clasped in prayer. Upon a wall, three swords hang while another embellishes the side of the tomb itself. The stained-glass window lighting the scene depicts a tableau of sacred benediction.

Revealed Aspects

Utter stillness pervades this image. It is one beyond the dictates of time, shut away from external influences. In accordance with the suit, it represents a period of rest from intellectual concerns or anxieties. The figure's praying hands and the window's theme of blessed healing do not demand a strictly religious interpretation. Instead, they emphasize the deeply meditative quality of the condition depicted and, more important, its curative purpose. The horizontal sword directly beneath the figure implies how this restorative phase is able to provide stabilization when existence becomes unmanageable.

Veiled Aspects

The figure of carved stone adorns a sarcophagus. As such, it symbolizes a respite profound enough to mimic death itself. The three swords point downward toward the sculpted subject. These can imply destructive outer forces from which a desperate escape is being attempted. However, an over-reliance upon deliberate isolation may lead to a life experienced through an armored cocoon. In such a state of eternal slumber, the true benediction available by a reasonable reprieve never happens. Alternately, this Pip in association with its element can illustrate a situation in which a needed recovery from mental stress never occurs or when a cut-off of communication takes place on an intellectual level.

Five of Swords

Description

A smiling figure holds two swords over his shoulder and points another downward into the shoreline upon which he stands. A further two lay at his feet. Closer to the turbulent water's edge, the backs of a pair of retreating forms can be seen beneath a cloud-filled sky.

Revealed Aspects

Even though the vanquisher has claimed center stage, what is unfolding involving the image's background figures may be equivalently significant. The two swords upon the sand can imply a voluntary submission. By this scenario, the defeated have thrown down their weapons in a refusal to partake in a confrontation with an opponent incapable of honorable warfare. Consequently, the rewards won in this clash will prove ultimately worthless. This is so since vileness displayed on the battlefield is an indicator of future mismanagement of ill-gotten gains by their eventual loss.

Veiled Aspects

Rare among any of the Tarot's largely impassive figures is a discernible facial expression. Therefore, this Pip is an exception indeed. Even so, the precise nature of the central figure's definite smile remains ambiguous. One interpretation might describe it as the satisfied smirk of a battle's victor while gloating at the losers' retreat. The suit and related element indicate a swift skirmish of a cerebral kind. The spoils to be had include the adding of four swords to the winner's own, hinting at a hording of intellectual power and control through non-physical methods. If this is so, it is not difficult to imagine the conqueror resorting to undignified, but clever measures to achieve his goal. Maybe this is why the furthest figure appears hunched over in dazed disbelief.

Six of Swords

Description

A man, woman, and child are traveling by boat. While the waters on one side of the barge are placid, those on the other ripple turbulently. The six upright swords piercing the vessel's floor do not hinder its movement.

Revealed Aspects

Once more, water serves to represents inner, emotional realms. Within the sphere of this suit, a voyage upon it indicates one concerning deeply intellectual matters. Surely, the sight of the six swords stuck into the boat's bottom is one of the most arresting found in all of the Pips. Furthermore, its extreme incongruity points decidedly toward a symbolic rather than literal interpretation. Although not specified explicitly, the swords in this somber context describe some type of immense negativity borne by a group—familial or otherwise. Nevertheless, through their combined strength, they are capable of maintaining an endurable balance as they journey through life together. Whilst still bearing the burden of the swords, the boat's maintenance of a steady course between both calm and undulating waters implies this.

Veiled Aspects

The element of air associated with this suit encompasses communication. Yet regardless of their relative proximity, the figures as depicted appear isolated from each other. The barge signifies a container holding them together as a unit in their shared misery. As such, it provides but a deceptively safe mode of transport only. The barge's confines have severed the group's ties from everyday existence and an ability to function as part of society. Furthermore, the familial dynamic suggests the passing down or even fostering of this wretchedness from one generation to the next. What is most ominous here is the trio's attempted flight from a destructive force. Indeed, the swords representing it not only outnumber the figures evenly by two to one, but also act as the boat's masthead, guiding them toward even greater disaster.

Seven of Swords

Description

With stealthy steps, a figure in turban and tunic carries away five swords. He is departing a tented encampment. Left behind are two additional swords that pierce the ground.

Revealed Aspects

There would seem little doubt as to the guilt of the sneaking figure in the crime he appears to be committing. Perhaps instead he is in the process of taking back goods wrongly stolen from him originally. As evidenced by the swords and the figure's gleeful expression, the accomplishment of this act happens by mental shrewdness as opposed to brute strength. Indeed, this coupled with the swiftness associated with the suit's element may be the crucial commodities his adversaries are lacking.

Veiled Aspects

A robbery is in progress. In the suit's realm, the absconded swords signify not so much physical plunder, but that which increases control of intellectual matters. This can include the ability to sway effectively others politically, morally, and ideologically. The rogue's exotic costume may have been required to complete successfully a traitorous infiltration of enemy territory. Furthermore, the pair of abandoned swords might represent some form of misdirection or cunning trap. The consequences of these deceptions will only further conceal the figure's connection to the theft and hinder his rivals' progress.

Eight of Swords

Description
Blindfolded and bound, a figure in crimson robes stands upon a marshland. Eight swords pierce the damp earth to stand vertically on either side. A formidable, red-roofed castle looms from a distant mountaintop.

Revealed Aspects
In height, width, and vertical position, there is a visual similarity between the scene's only human figure and the inanimate objects surrounding it. This deliberate likeness stresses their essential correlation as depicting ideas of a double-edged nature. Even if nobly intended, sometimes radical beliefs carry a formidable price when they counter the seat of mainstream thought signified by the castle. So then the figure's acceptance of her fate is worthy of a martyr in its absolute conviction of purpose. That the results may entail ostracism and loss of command on the physical plane is of little concern. For far above the stony fortress, the purity of her vision soars.

Veiled Aspects
One of the most unsettling tableaus of the Minor Arcana, its restrained figure and threatening swords illustrate the suit's complex issues of intellectual control and communication. The superficial link between the color of the robes and the castle rooftops may hint at a deeper connection. For perhaps the captive once held dominion over the turreted stronghold. If so, a separation now exists between the figure and the decision-making processes so common to the suit. A further strengthening of the subject's isolation represents a negative aspect of the relevant element. This limiting situation may have been self-inflicted through

the figure's own prejudices and outmoded ways of thinking connoted by the blindfold and bindings.

Nine of Swords

Description

As if awoken from a terrifying dream in the dead of night, a figure sits upright with open hands pressed to its face. A carving depicting a battle scene of some kind decorates the side of the bedstead. Nine swords hang horizontally upon the wall.

Revealed Aspects

A positive interpretation of the scene might perceive it as representing a decisive instant of realization leading to change. Indeed, this insight can entail the acceptance of one's own culpability in the troublesome situation resulting in the turmoil illustrated by the Pip. Alternatively, the card may even simply signify the relief one experiences when startled awake from a nightmare only to comprehend the folly of the fear it had produced. However, even if proven groundless, such nocturnal disturbances often serve as a warning from the psyche of something amiss demanding further exploration.

Veiled Aspects

This disquieting image portrays a universally familiar moment of personal anguish. Symbolically, the multiple swords set against utter blackness indicate the suit's harmful mental processes when uncontrolled. Excessive worry, grief, and guilt are capable of consuming and even misdirecting an existence away from optimal functioning toward self-destruction. The violent bedstead carving may suggest a specific conflict or series of disputes between the tormented figure and another party causing the unrest. So caught between the battalion of threatening swords above and the carved tableau of pain below, this victim suffers alone through an endless night.

Ten of Swords

Description

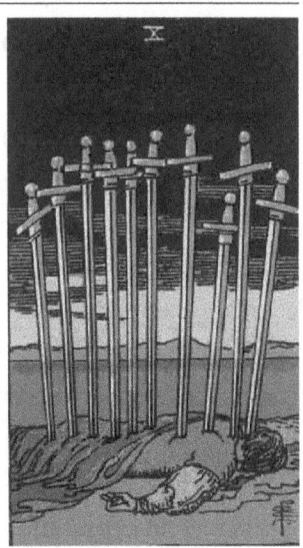

Beneath a darkling sky, ten swords pierce the back of a fallen figure with its face turned away. One visible hand appears to be forming a signal.

Revealed Aspects

This horrifying tableau might serve well as the finale to a tragedy for the stage. Indeed, the black sky seems to be falling curtain-like from the heavens. So at least superficially, the possibility of any action beyond this point seems unlikely at best. Nevertheless, perhaps the horizon's glowing yellow is heralding a rising sun. The prone figure cannot be any closer to the ground—symbolizing the foundation of his beliefs—than as shown. In this context, the illustration depicts martyrdom to convictions controversial enough to illicit a devastating response. Here, the swords represent contrary opinions wielded by the sufferer's detractors. While these may have succeeded in killing off any revolutionary ideas temporarily, the selfless act will provide inspiration for future likeminded individuals. Maybe then the ambiguous hand gesture is one communicating survival.

Veiled Aspects

Given the suit's associations, the Pip focuses upon a situation of non-physical assault. The backstabbing nature of the attack and multiple swords indicate an underhanded endeavor executed by a group. In accordance with the suit's element and darker attributes, this was a swift and therefore perhaps unanticipated assault accomplished through intellectual manipulation and deviousness. Alternately, the supposed victim might have initiated the assault through ideas deliberately formulated to antagonize. In this way, the target is now the ironic source for the very same destructive thoughts with injurious results. That the figure's position renders it faceless emphasizes how identifying the wounded party is of less import than recognizing of the damaging act itself.

Pentacles

Frequently employed in magical practices, the pentacle is a protective amulet formed in the shape of a pentagram or five-pointed star. Here we will view each of the points as representing one of the four elements, with the fifth etheric one indicating spirit, their source and unifier. Thus, the pentacle diagram symbolizes the appearance of the Divine through the joining of and in conjunction with the elements. In the same way, the Major Arcana might be viewed as the Tarot's fifth or quintessential element with the Minor Arcana suits corresponding to the other four. So then, one of the Pentacles' most significant messages is the many ways the numinous manifests itself in the earthbound territories. Therefore, the pentacles seen in the following images frequently serve as physical objects or actually form part of the manmade or natural settings. Being attentive to the outwardly mundane can reveal profound links between them and the Divine. Even so, it should be noted how often in early Tarot decks with non-illustrated Pips, the icon for this division is a coin, indicating the suit's concerns with the material sphere.

Earth is associated with the suit of Pentacles. Various forms of practicality, material productiveness, nature, and sensory experiences express this element. The spectrum of personality traits and situation characterizers illustrated within this division of the Tarot associated with this element range from: protectiveness to abandonment or indifference; generosity to greediness or wastefulness; and steadfastness to obstinacy or recklessness. Also implied by the element of earth, these qualities are stable and thus resistant to change in nature. In magical tradition, various land animals are associated with earth and so will be shown intermittently in the following cards. With the suit's flower- and fruit-filled scenes, the characteristics categorized energetically as feminine connected with Pentacles can be possessed by anyone in varying degrees. A few examples of actual locales in which events indicative of the suit commonly unfold include, but are not limited to: an industrial workplace; a trade school; a garden, woodland, farm, or agricultural setting; or any place of apprenticeship.

King of Pentacles

Description

A King resides upon a throne adorned with bulls' heads festooned with garlands. Such nature imagery as flowers, fruit, leaves, and vines cover his crown and robes. While in one hand he raises an orb-capped scepter, the other displays a large pentacle. From beneath his robes, one extended, armored foot is placed upon a foot-rest bearing a carved animal face. A castle can be seen in the distance from the verdant garden wherein the monarch rules.

Revealed Aspects

When combined, the finest aspects of this King make him the dream father. Generous, good-humored, and a superlative provider, he is the master of the Minor Arcana's division of natural abundance, as shown by the various symbols of flora and fauna. The suit's icon and castle represent the products of his unmatched business acumen and resultant monetary success. The symbolic sexual union of the orb-capped scepter attests to his amatory prowess. Furthermore, the armored foot emerging from ornate robes indicates the stalwart personal code guiding an outward charitableness. The appearance of this Court card can describe a situation of plentiful success in the home, office, or romantic affair. It may also imply one in which reality-based paternal guidance is given or received.

Veiled Aspects

The luxuriant pattern of the King's robes resembles so closely the surrounding garden, it is nearly impossible to discern their separation.

This can show the King's downfall when his best traits become overgrown. Such a change often manifests itself by an inability or deliberate refusal to respect the boundaries between personal and professional life. Alternatively, by extension, he may develop into the disloyal lover who respects passion's demands sooner than a faithful pledge to any individual. Moreover, the potential exists for either the exaggeration or decay of the King's ethical code into tyrannical stubbornness or carnal abandon, as represented by the animal emblems. This card can indicate a period of excessive demands from work or office, or a time when the stresses between these bases become unmanageable. It can also connote a phase when basic needs are not given or received, or when ego-driven debauchery prevents the use of common sense in familial or professional responsibilities.

Queen of Pentacles

Description

Within a flowering bower, a Queen clasps a pentacle in both hands. A full-length green veil depends from a floral motif crown to envelop her red gown. Engravings of leafy, fruit-laden branches of a pear tree, goats' heads, and horned cherubs enrich her throne. A ruddy-colored hare leaps in the foreground of this woodland tableau adorned with flowers, rivers, and mountains.

Revealed Aspects

As if watching over a cherished child upon her knee, the Queen looks down lovingly upon the pentacle held in her hands. She is the ultimate earth mother, as indicated by the lush bower, rivers, and the grassy green hue of her enveloping veil. With two feet resting directly upon the exposed earth, she connects profoundly to the suit's element. As such, her firm grounding in the workings of daily life results in a monarch who is sensible, honest, and supremely self-sufficient. The fruited branches, goats' heads, and hare symbolize her earthy sexuality and industrious disposition. The horned elemental earth spirits may represent those dependent upon her extensive everyday knowledge, or possibly the numerous maternal tasks she undertakes routinely with easy adeptness. The appearance of this Court card implies a nurturing situation in which a giving or receiving of straightforward advice or priceless knowledge takes place. It can signify a phase of prolific productivity or stability at home.

Veiled Aspects

When shadows of ineptitude, self-doubt, or egotism prevent the sun from reaching the Queen's bower, her flowery dominion may decompose. If this occurs, the cherubs' ceaseless demands overwhelm a Queen unqualified for the title. Similarly, tendencies toward the goats' unappeasable appetites and the hare's mindless reproduction may topple her crown. Consequently, she becomes an incompetent sovereign exhibiting little self-control, while remaining unaware of her own uselessness. This card can suggest a seemingly enforced situation of monotonous drudgery, especially a domestic one benefiting everyone but the doer. It may also connote continued failed efforts at either giving or accepting maternal wisdom of a practical nature.

Knight of Pentacles

Description
A Knight in full armor sits astride a still horse. The two have paused along an expanse of deeply plowed earth. The Knight holds a pentacle aloft. Oak leaves top both the rider's helmet and the steed's headpiece.

Revealed Aspects
In contrast to the other three Knights shown in some form of movement, the horseman here appears to be motionless. This implies those positive traits closely associated with the classic Knight figure of lore, especially evident in this combination of suit and element—most notably, fidelity, single-mindedness, and dependability. Furthermore, he is committed to a cause by unshakable faith. His using the pentacle itself as guide and devotional icon shows this. The inclusion of the oak leaves implies the potentiality for ample growth through what may seem to be unhurried progress. Consequently, in order to achieve a particular destination, even of the spiritual kind, the Knight suggests taking a well-established travel route as opposed to an unknown one. This card can typify reliance upon tested methods for a guaranteed outcome. Likewise, it can point to those times when resolute belief provides the strength needed to complete a desired quest.

Veiled Aspects
While upholding the values of a daily crusade, the Knight must be ready to think and act independently as well. There is an adherence to meaningless obligation when this does not occur. So then, the plowed earth illustrates how the enduring Knight's undoing is dormant in his most advantageous attributes. A detrimental cycle begins with a lack of

enthusiasm or ingenuity; leading to uncertainty, judgment errors, and loss of self-worth; and then finally, to rote behavior or blind allegiance. Accordingly, the figure's full-armored uniform lends him a robotic appearance. In the same way, the outcome of an inability to pursue any form of goal with discipline and resourcefulness is indolence or a squandering of resources through unrestraint. This card can describe a situation in which a pursuit is spoiled or abandoned, particularly of an entrepreneurial kind, through laziness, a lack of personal conviction, or self-indulgence.

Page of Pentacles

Description

A Page stands upon a grassy stretch of land. Small flowers bloom about his feet. In both hands, he raises a pentacle as if to study it more intently. In the distance, a portion of the ground displays the marks of a plow.

Revealed Aspects

As indicated by the figure's suit, rank, and element, this Page is concerned with gaining education through dedicated service, primarily in the professional and domestic arenas. The tiny flowers at his feet symbolize this recent blooming of such knowledge. Their growth is dependent upon the intensity of his examination of and commitment to the pentacle—the suit's icon representing here whatever the given area of study might be. The small patch of plowed earth implies the Page's dawning acceptance of effort and perseverance as sure methods to achieving goals. This card may herald a period of intense learning, most frequently in the form of business-related training or home economics, in order to better one's quality of life.

Veiled Aspects

Few shortcuts exist in reaching mastery in any field. When the Page deludes himself into believing otherwise, he will attain certain failure with rapid ease. Ironically, success could happen with the constructive use of energy typically reserved for devising complicated schemes to avoid serious effort. His is the regrettable case of the delinquent whose clashes early on in school or occupation self-perpetuate a downward fall. Moreover, without a caring instructor or supervisor providing needed guidance, the Page will be led irrevocably astray. The appearance of this Court card may announce the start of learning difficulties on the job, or a lack of adaptability to function in a specific employment or home environment.

Ace of Pentacles

Description
A rose hedge from which an opening is trimmed borders a luxuriant, lily-filled garden. Through it can be seen tall, mountain peaks. There is an offering of a pentacle above the idyllic scene.

Revealed Aspects
The ovoid shape of the garden portal is reminiscent of the laurel wreath of The World trump, and even The Fool's numerical digit of zero. At least initially, these mystical associations might seem incongruous with the principally secular concerns of the suit. However, at the same time, the realm of this Ace hints at the potential for spiritual richness suffusing everyday life, the physical aspects of existence, and especially nature. Indeed, the pentacle itself symbolizes mystical completion—as discussed earlier, its five points indicating the meeting of the four earthly elements with the Divine. As suggested by the hand's giving gesture, such celestial resources are readily available to those with an awareness of them.

Veiled Aspects
Seeing the distant mountains through the hedge opening itself reinforces the revelation of the unexpected numinous quality of this Ace's realm. This is not surprising when viewing these peaks as representative of the goal of the transformative quest. As already described in the Trumps, reaching this aim requires challenges in both the psychic and earthly worlds, the latter embodied especially in this suit. Therefore, when a desire to bypass these necessary efforts taints this realm, it becomes one abounding with greed, malfunction, and corruption. Since the most

valuable aspects of this Ace's gift are buried within the outwardly mundane, they will yield no benefit to those demanding them without a sincere respect for their worth.

Two of Pentacles

Description

A youthful figure juggles two pentacles whilst standing on one foot. The objects appear within a lemniscate symbol. In the distance, the rolling waves of the sea toss about two ships.

Revealed Aspects

Tremendous dexterity and balance are required of the scene's performer. In this context, the lemniscate infinity symbol suggests a limitless resource to these qualities. Just as the ships they mirror, the figure's considerable skills enable the accomplishment of varied tasks simultaneously. A more literal translation of the illustration connotes a situation in which one finds self-worth and a sense of wonder in simpler pleasures. It may also suggest the successful entertainment of others.

Veiled Aspects

A darker interpretation of the same image finds the figure near collapse. Demanded either by the self or outside forces, the laborious balancing act has become a tiresome or even impossible routine. So then here, the lemniscate symbol signifies the endless repetition of unconstructive behaviors for reasons no longer relevant or even remembered. Since in many cases these actions benefit others only and not the individual, they have the potential of generating overpowering resentment. Additionally, and in accordance with the embodied nature of the suit and element, the negative aspects of this card can include cycles of unhealthy physical masochism and substance abuse of all kinds.

Three of Pentacles

Description

A young apprentice pauses in his work on the tracery for some form of sacred building. The ornamental design incorporates three pentacles. Two superiors scrutinize the completed work. One of the inspectors compares this to a set of plans.

Revealed Aspects

The novice here represents anyone in a position of training. As such, the superiors depicted must assess his output. Furthermore and as implied by the plans, accomplishing such often takes place within guidelines set by those more knowledgeable. In order for this dynamic to operate productively, the underling must respect the overseers and value the demanded task. Unquestionably then, the apprentice must be possessed of an unwavering faith in order to succeed. Perhaps this is why the setting is churchlike in appearance.

Veiled Aspects

Characteristic of the suit and associated element, the qualities of patience and persistence are essential in completing the type of craftwork shown. Furthermore, the pentacles' elevated placement in this holy space signifies the attainment of a spiritual goal through what at least outwardly may seem tediously repetitive. Therefore, no true achievement of personal aspiration happens when the learner refuses to make a complete and dedicated commitment. An apathetic or combative approach will surely prevent an individual from functioning constructively within a group as illustrated by the trio; and most especially so when judgement from supervisors is required.

Four of Pentacles

Description

A seated figure looks directly forward. Four large pentacles are positioned about his person—two beneath his feet and another atop the crown he is wearing. The forth is held fast in his arms. In the distance, there appears the skyline of a tower-filled city.

Revealed Aspects

Whether due to noble birth or self-made success, the figure is one wielding considerable authority as signified by his crown. The suit and element specify this supremacy as originating in material wealth, perhaps illustrated by the city. In addition, it is by this affluence he identifies himself and functions so effectively in the world. The balanced placement of the pentacles atop the crown and beneath the feet declares the long-standing establishment of his success. While simultaneously, the deliberate, shield-like use of the forth one suggests the strength and protection these afford him.

Veiled Aspects

No part of the image's subject makes physical contact with his dominion—not even his feet touch the earth. At the same time, the topmost pentacle dwarfs the crown to connote a complete preoccupation with maintaining his fortunes. Such a mindset has the potential to deteriorate into one of tremendous greed justified by a distorted concern for self-preservation at the reckless expense of others. The vast space between the figure and the city represents ironically the resultant detachment between the two.

Five of Pentacles

Description

Two miserable figures make their way through a raging snowstorm. One is a crippled beggar, equipped with crutches and a bell tied around his neck. The other struggles shoeless through the white drifts, one of her feet bandaged. The warm glow of a church-like building's stained-glass window featuring five pentacles lights their way.

Revealed Aspects

At least by initial observation, it would seem doubtful to uncover a single uplifting element in this desperate tableau. Moreover, while the realistic hardships depicted symbolically specify the suit's negative potential for material loss, the relevant element indicates the longstanding nature of such adversity. So then, the golden window above the figures' heads represents a non-corporeal form of sustenance providing enduring strength. Most obviously, both organized religion and private faith offer an abundance of spiritual satisfaction. As an extension of this idea, the appearance of the pentacles within the stained-glass design may be a means of elevating the icon and its implications to mystical status. In this way, industrious work or even mundane tasks when performed in an effective and committed manner can provide inner-illumination. In accordance with this interpretation, the figures need not look to the sacred window itself as they pass, since it is but an externalized projection of this internal source of fortitude.

Veiled Aspects

Consumed by their own plight, both figures hurry by what might provide them with the relief they urgently require. This is so since a fixed concentration upon the material world alone as the meaning of existence has rendered them spiritually blind. Here, the crutches and bell provide props for extracting sympathy and summoning continual assistance from others. The two shun the sanctuary since its mystical riches may require a level of selflessness each is unwilling to give. Consequently, until they are prepared to be responsible for their own wellbeing, this woebegone pair will remain crippled souls hobbling through a frozen wasteland.

Six of Pentacles

Description

Two beggars kneel at the feet of a man of greater means. The latter holds a perfectly balanced scale in one hand whilst dispensing golden coins in the other. Six pentacles adorn the air surrounding him.

Revealed Aspects

Ironic yet admirable, there is a certain nobility to be found in the supplicants' pleading gestures. For they signify a comprehension and beneficial acceptance of one's subservient position in certain situations. These include those in which one seeks improvement from a sensible master in a group setting. The balanced scale used in the distribution of the coins between the two kneeling figures infers the sage's impartiality. In this context and that of the suit, the pentacles can betoken practical wisdom or training imparted in a long-hallowed fashion. The initiate's intentional surrender often requires a public relinquishment of the ego or one's valued place in the world as shown in the scene. Nevertheless, the very air surrounding the trio is alive with the potential mystical treasures available to all involved in the process. Quite subtly, the relationship between fledgling novice and illuminated sage echoes the cyclical role exchange between the Fool and the transformed being of The World trump in the repetition of the Tarot journey.

Veiled Aspects

There is a selfish and unfair wielding of power when equilibrium is lost. The scale allows the precise meting out of the gold as illustrated. However, the beggars will not be provided with a single coin more than is absolutely due them. The central figure's corruption blocks any sympathy for the genuinely underprivileged or, when relevant, recognition of his disadvantaged origins prior to the current success being misused. The tragic flaw of such hardheartedness is assuming wealth founded in materialism alone somehow endures longer than poverty. Conversely, this Pip can suggest the indiscriminate giving away of basic resources regardless of decent intentions, or the senseless wasting of what is received in good faith.

Seven of Pentacles

Description
Pentacles adorn a mass of leafy greenery. Nearby is the man who has been cultivating their growth. He pauses in his work to ascertain what has developed.

Revealed Aspects
No matter how intensive, completing a project requires more than the actual labor directed toward it. For then the unavoidable moment will arrive when patience will be mandatory above all else. Heavy with the suit's icon, the vines represent the flourishing of a practical plan requiring direct, if not physical interaction. As represented by the resting figure, the value of a constructive waiting process is in considering one's achievement thus far. That knowledge allows efficient planning for the next phase. As exemplified by its essential import to cloistered life, the joining of manual effort and contemplation produce a realistic foundation from which mystical flight may more readily happen.

Veiled Aspects
Be it fruit, flower, or business venture, the benefits of optimum growing conditions and the most earnest of tending can all be undermined in a moment of premature harvesting. Worse still is forcing a yield without an initial planting requiring time, effort, and resources. These unwise attempts most commonly result in impulsive decision-making masquerading as an eagerness to move forward. Similar damage can be wrought when involved parties are not respected enough to be consulted before action is taken. Sometimes, the impetuous individual rejects others' work methods based on self-serving claims of their

ineffectualness. When in reality, what is truly the cause is intolerance for any means of operating not conforming to one's own in terms of method or timetable.

Eight of Pentacles

Description
Armed with hammer and chisel, a seated craftsman engraves the design of a large pentacle using a workbench for support. The results of similar efforts hang upon the wall before him. The rooftops of a nearby town rise in the background.

Revealed Aspects
The evident care and skill with which the figure produces a tangible output clearly expresses the suit and element. The engraving of the pentacle design shows an imbuing of the task with mystical import. The numerous examples of the finished product speak of the artisan's productivity and satisfaction with what he achieves on a daily basis. This Pip can represent further a mutually beneficial scenario wherein all of the participants in a practical course of action operate efficiently and with reciprocal respect.

Veiled Aspects
Although within reach, the craftsman and his bench appear to be a considerable distance from the town. This may stand for the remoteness experienced by an individual whose function society demeans. This bias results in the belittlement of the same dependable worker by those benefiting directly from such reliable efforts. Still, the man may toil on while possibly jeopardizing his health and well-being, until being consumed by eventual disillusionment of a life wasted. Alternatively, but just as detrimental is the person refusing to endure the drudgery often required in moving toward a goal—and within this suit, one perhaps promising either materials or spiritual rewards.

Nine of Pentacles

Description

An exquisitely robed woman of apparent means or noble rank pauses in her bountiful, private garden. A hand rests upon one pentacle among the nine seemingly growing from a fruited vine. Upon the other gloved one, a hooded falcon perches and is the subject of her gaze. A snail is making its way across the lady's path.

Revealed Aspects

Not strictly indicating societal position, the high standing of the woman signifies instead an evolved state of being. The blooming pentacles are the practical commodities resulting from this internal advancement of which others may partake and benefit. Two representatives from the animal world closely linked to this nature-based suit suggest the Pip's further crucial messages. In its stately progress whilst traveling wide distances, the typically unobserved snail represents perseverance to a goal with seeming ease. The hooded falcon connotes the capacity to conserve perfected skills until needed. Her gloved hand implies the ability to withstand the claws of daily existence capable of disturbing a less evolved being. Blissful in her solitude, the mistress of this Pip has achieved such mastery largely on her own.

Veiled Aspects

A darker view offers a different perspective of the same scene. In it, the lady's hand upon the pentacle becomes a selfish clutching to prevent sharing of any kind. Even her animal minions reveal far less noble qualities in this nighttime garden. The snail is now a token of indolence leaving a despicable trail of unfulfilled potential. As for the bird of prey, its hooded state may imply either a blinding egocentrism or an existence so rarefied as to become ultimately uninformed in its exclusion of everyday life. Whichever the case, both stand for the wasting of genuine talents of potential worth to many.

Ten of Pentacles

Description

A variety of figures populates a street scene. Two adults converse contentedly. From around one of them, a small child peers at an elderly man in a robe embellished with mystical symbols. Two dogs are attracted to the sage figure as well. A castle and balanced scales decorate a nearby wall.

Revealed Aspects

Disillusionment, sarcasm, and self-doubt—for many adults, these are the customary qualities affecting perception, and thus dictators of one's actions. This is not so for the child or dogs as shown. Indicative of the suit, they function instead in accordance with a worldview based on sensation, instinct, unconditional love, and inexhaustible potential. Wrapped in his mysterious cloak, the wise man proves the potential persistence of such a magical and largely optimistic outlook into old age. The Pip's element suggests nature as the source of the tools to achieve this sadly uncommon trait. By it, a productive existence benefits others. Even though personal contentment will follow as a byproduct of such a giving nature, considering one's own needs is just as necessary.

Veiled Aspects

So preoccupied with discussing the day's minutiae, the chatting couple remain oblivious to the extraordinary encounter unfolding between the children, animals, and the sage. If allowed, life's inescapable petty rivalries, minor disappointments, and trifling grievances can consume any appreciation for the true wonder of being. The arcane symbols adorning the elder figure's robe and the material-based wall images emphasize the fundamental dichotomy explored in the card. Available to all, they represent a choice between the two as to how one may proceed in this world.

III
The Inner Path

What can not be known remains unknowable, yet I see with the eye of the sun as if it came to rest on my forehead, throwing light in the dark corners of things, casting the shadows of men into uncharted lands.

—Normandi Ellis, *Awakening Osiris: A New Translation of the Egyptian Book of the Dead*[54]

---

54 Ellis, *Awakening Osiris.*

Finding the Way

Originating in the late 1950s and still relevant today, a "happening" is a term describing a particular type of artistic event. These occasions feature simultaneous performances from a variety of disciplines, such as music, dance, art, and drama. Both improvisation and audience participation are encouraged to result in a fully immersive aesthetic experience. Because of their singular nature, no two such events are ever alike or repeatable. In essence, a happening is a *living* art form.

Our understanding of the Tarot self-reading process entails many of the same core elements, while referring back to the previously given general definition of divination—that is, accessing hidden information—as a starting point. At its most basic, self-divination with cards can be viewed as an exchange between the reader, the deck, and deeper wisdom. So then what results might be termed a triologue. Even more so, a transformative reading involves soul-touching—a happening in which a profound communion takes place between yourself and the source of that deeper truth through the cards. Author and mystic Shani Oates notes:

> Prophesie is the oracular medium by which we may engage with the "other," a sentience beyond the impedimenta of time, context, circumstance or consequence. Subliminal absorption into this stream of gnosis is startlingly direct, ambivalent and amoral. Once apprehended, it is our very human comprehension that interprets the missives perceived there; where our own intuitive skills garner the individual context dedicated to that fixed moment of the reading.[55]

View the self-reading session as a uniquely intimate moment capable of profound reverberations joining mind, heart, and soul, while unifying

---

55 Shani Oates, correspondence with author, August 2016.

inner and outer realities. The process will call into application nearly every aspect of you. It is an opportunity to integrate your sensitivity and intellect, book learning, individual and group training, regular practice with cards, and perhaps other forms of contemplation and meditation—all to be expressed with improvisational skill during the self-reading. Your earnest dedication to the work obliged by this private adventure into highly subjective territories will determine the depth of the results. This is especially so for the majority of us whose access to deeper realms may not occur with effortless ease.

Just as with the most effective "happenings," the reading experience operates in a realm bypassing the restrictions of the intellect to summon forth the mysteries of the heart. Demanding definitive answers or specific future information from the cards negates your free will to effect change. Furthermore, such expectations take a strictly forward-moving view of time, ignoring the dynamic interaction between past, present, and potentialities. In the card reading process, let us abandon a standard, strictly forward-moving view of time in most instances. Spiritual writer and instructor, Llewellyn Vaughan-Lee explains, "If we live in the past or the future, in our memories or expectations, we are firmly caught in the illusion of time and the dance of shadows. Only in the present moment do we have access to our eternal Self, which is outside of time."[56]

The most productive sessions are those concerned less with the "whys" of existence and more with the motivations and situations directly linked to you. It is through a self-reading's exploration of them that the reasons so often hunted for are uncovered. From these revelations, fruitful guidance of genuine value and real transformation flow.

---

56   Llewellyn Vaughan-Lee, *The Paradoxes of Love* (Inverness, 1996).

Do not fear this unique experience which can be, in unequal parts, thrilling, challenging, elating, frustrating, and sometimes even unexpectedly humorous. Certainly, this is a process calling for practice and continual exploration to achieve fluidity. Moreover, there will never likely be a consensually agreed upon answer as to how precisely divination can achieve its aims so effectively. Vaughan-Lee affirms, "The heart reveals what the mind can hardly grasp."[57] Those who have experienced a transformative self-reading can attest to the genuine benefits of lifting the veils to unexpected understanding. Still, no reading is ever truly finished. For an enlightening session can continue to unfold toward increasingly profound meaning and burn on as impetus toward unanticipated growth well afterwards.

More than anything, the Tarot's images and a sincerely performed self-reading reflect the very *experience* of living—from its most mundane episodes to those of glittering revelation. Let us value these openings to awakening and rely upon the wisdom of our hearts to illuminate them all in a glorious light.

Preparing for the Inner Path

Many a novice will concern themselves with the sometimes elaborate reading preparations suggested before a session. Although in many instances worthwhile, such preliminary ceremonies are not mandatory. Instead, it is crucial to achieve a composed and receptive state for the self-reading process at hand. For if you are relaxed, the all-important connections between the cards will be more apparent, the facility to

---

[57] Ibid. British occultist Dion Fortune (1890-1946) states: "…divination, taken in its true sense, is spiritual diagnosis, a very different matter to fortune-telling." Learn more in the following book: Dion Fortune, *The Mystical Qabalah* (York Beach, 2000).

receive their messages readily available, and the overall experience that much more energized.

So then, do implement whatever contributes to a sense of peaceful openness. Varying according to individual needs, this may range from the simple lighting of a candle to the more complex practice of deck consecration and cleansing rituals. While the former are most often used to prepare a new deck, the latter purport to clear away negative energies some believe attach themselves to the cards in the course of a difficult reading. Others will store their decks in specially designed bags or boxes. Once again, while not denigrating any of these choices, they remain exactly that—choices. More indispensable is the calm-inducing effect of the procedures themselves. Spiritual teacher Swami Kriyananda[58] reminds us, "True intuition can never come when we're in a state of emotional turmoil."[59]

Therefore, there should be no hesitation to read upon a preferred surface or during a particular time of day. Light a favorite candle and investigate breathing techniques for relaxation. Or else perhaps start a session by making a symbolic gesture to represent the aspect of the Tarot reading as a "happening" experience. For example, randomly scatter a few favorite stones, crystals, or shells into a bowl kept nearby. Just as your reading, the pattern they create is incapable of random replication again. Furthermore, do not hesitate to invoke otherworldly sources of guidance to oversee the session should this be part of your spiritual belief system.

Nevertheless, reading with little or no preparation on occasion can provide a balancing antidote to potential rigidity. One of the definitive

---

58 Swami Kriyananda (born James Donald Walters) was born in Teleajen, Romania in 1926 and died in Assisi, Italy in 2013.
59 J. Donald Walters, *Intuition for Starters: How to Know and Trust Your Inner Guidance* (Nevada City, 2002).

goals of any new skill is to reach a level of proficiency when creativity can flow unimpeded by technical concerns. Adequate preparation, with allowances for spontaneity, can assist in reaching this desired state.

Newcomers and professionals alike find tremendous value in Tarot journaling. The scope of this noncompulsory practice can range from noting personal thoughts about individual cards to detailed reading analyses. As for the latter, oftentimes a deeper comprehension of a session happens with the actual process of committing your thoughts on it to paper. It is also a revealing developmental gauge to compare conclusions made about an earlier session with those gained after the benefit of further contemplation and reading experience.

The terms meditation and contemplation are defined in a myriad of ways, contain many similarities, and are performed according to a multitude of systems. Both strive toward clarifying and elevating consciousness. An objective common among many meditative practices is to still the mind through rigorous training. Combined with numerous techniques, this can entail directing active thought away from prolonged attention on any one thing. Meditation contrasts with the practice of contemplation which can involve the active reflection upon a particular object, concept, idea, or quality.

Every Tarot card can be used for productive contemplation alone. Yet, an ideal initial step for those interested in the deck's divinatory possibilities would to first become familiar with each card through a contemplation of it. Occultist and author, Julian Vayne notes, "The cards are seventy eight distinct personalities, seventy eight spirits to make friends with. Get to know them, so that divination can become a fluent conversation between the denizens of the archetypal Deep Mind which they represent, and consciousness."[60] Allow these new

---

60 Julian Vayne, correspondence with author, August 2016.

acquaintances to evolve into trusted comrades—and then deeper still, to become astral doorways through which you may encounter unanticipated and profound truths.[61]

As will be seen, the self-reading method to follow will strongly promote thoughtful and creative concentration, discouraging rote memorization of the suggested interpretations. Indeed and as already seen, preferred here is the term "message" over "meaning," the latter more commonly employed in card divination. "Message" implies communication—in this context, between various aspects of the self in contemplation and even different dimensions of existence. Authority on the visual poetry of the Tarot, Enrique Enriquez asserts, "By perceiving a message in Tarot cards, we create a new meaning for the cards every time we observe them…"[62]

Contemplation sessions with a Tarot card need not be longer than fifteen minutes to a half-hour at most. Make sure to undertake these undisturbed and well-rested, lest drowsiness interfere. Sit in a comfortable position, with a card either held in the hand or perhaps propped up on a table. Certainly, a single card will provide ample material for more than one session. Relate the focus of the contemplation primarily to the self—

---

61 The Hermetic Order of the Golden Dawn noted earlier utilized images and symbols as such astral doorways in their meditation practices influenced by Eastern esotericism. Mélusine Draco, *The Dictionary of Magic and Mystery* (Hants, 2012).

62 Enrique Enriquez, *Looking at the Marseilles Tarot: Notes on Tarot's Optical Language* (Colchester, 2007). Chilean film director, comparative religion scholar, and Tarot reader Alejandro Jodorowsky describes the deck as "a metaphysical machine" and "one of humanity's first optical languages." Alejandro Jodorowsky, Rachael LeValley, trans., *Psychomagic: The Transformative Power of Shamanic Psychotherapy* (Rochester, 2010).

to an inner aspect or imbalance of concern, or to a mode of behavior or everyday life situation expressed in the particular card's image. What follows are several suggestions as to how to use the cards for productive contemplation:

- Choose a "revealed" message from a single card and contemplate how it indicates: a recent or emergent understanding of benefit to you, a positive inner aspect to be encouraged, or the key to resolving a current imbalance.
- Choose a "veiled" message from a single card and contemplate how it indicates: a recent or emergent understanding detrimental to you since it has been overlooked, misinterpreted, or blocked; a negative inner aspect to be released; or the negative source of a recent or ongoing imbalance.

Determining the Route

Decide upon the spread to be utilized by setting an intention at the start of a session. This determination forms the foundation upon which the self-reading is constructed. Following here are tips to articulating this goal:

- Assist setting the intention by allowing a moment of unrushed, quiet contemplation to do so.
- From the spreads to be provided, select the one most appropriate for the intention identified, such as a particular imbalance or situation needing clarity. All spreads can be adjusted to focus on more specific concerns or aspects before the cards are drawn.
- While embracing past and potential realities, the spreads are designed largely to address present concerns.
- Alternatively, use an "open reading" by which no particular subject is focused on at the outset. Instead, what is sought here is guidance needed most at the moment of the self-reading. During an open reading, the identification of an imbalance or concern directly or indirectly affecting you most often emerges. This type of self-reading will provide you with a more objective view of a current

situation overall, while calling upon the past and looking toward the future concurrently. Open readings will work best with the spreads of possessing a broader scope; these include: Imbalance I.D., Past-Present-Future, Arch Bridge, Heart of the Matter, and Soul of the Matter.

- Regardless of the session's intention or spread utilized, you may choose to dedicate the outcome as one best for your greater good and that of all it might embrace.

Shuffling and Cutting the Cards

Numerous shuffling and cutting methods abound. The choice belongs to you. Discover your favorite techniques through test trials and practical application. Experimentation with them is encouraged in order to discover what provides the most personally satisfactory result. The following is a simple and efficient shuffling and cutting method.

Begin by placing the deck picture-facedown upon the center of the reading surface. Then shuffle the cards in any preferred standard or non-standard method. Concentrate on the reading's intention during this action. In the case of an open reading, simply calm the mind, assisted by a few full breaths, to promote a receptive state. After thoroughly mixing the cards, gather them back into a single pile, all the while maintaining their facedown position.

Next, take the single pile, using either hand, to cut it into three smaller ones of approximately equal size. Achieve this by lifting the pack just above the reading surface and then releasing each of the smaller piles (A, B, and C) in succession from the bottom of the deck. Place these in any desired pattern: for example, in a straight line from left-to-right or vice versa. Once this is completed, the three piles are restacked to form a single pile once more.

Most important here is to avoid reforming the deck into its pre-cut order by stacking the three smaller piles in the exact reverse order of their earlier distribution. This inadvertent error will nullify the deck cutting altogether. To avoid this, restack the cut cards in the following order: pick up pile A and place it on top of pile C; then place the pile consisting of A and C combined upon pile B to form a single pack. Now repeat the shuffling and cutting procedure. No more than three times is necessary to finish. In addition to assuring a complete mixing of the cards, the preceding process performed calmly can deepen a desired state of focused concentration.

Next, take the shuffled and cut deck to spread the cards upon the reading surface picture-facedown. This can be done easily in such patterns as a single horizontal line or semi-circle with an upward or downward arc. The cards are now ready to be drawn. Once this is completed, the remainder of the deck can be left where it is should additional cards be drawn later in the reading, or it can be gathered back into a single pile to be set aside.

Reversals

One of the goals of a keener perspective is to see beyond obvious, outer perceptions to hidden, inner understanding. To achieve this, one may attempt to accept the light and dark in all—others, situations, as well as ourselves—since these seemingly separate and often clashing aspects are actually expressions of the greater whole. Llewellyn Vaughan-Lee reminds us, "Embracing these contradictions with love and acceptance, we follow them to the source…pairs of opposites create the dance of life, the unending dance that comes from the unmanifest, inner world, onto the stage of manifestation."[63]

Such an all-encompassing viewpoint is directly analogous to card reading. During the shuffling process, a random top-to-bottom turning

---

63 Vaughan-Lee, *Paradoxes*.

of the cards takes place. So when the cards are selected, a percentage of them are reversed or upside-down. According to widely-used card reading methods, when reversals are observed, the interpretation of these upside-down cards is the opposite or, most typically, negative version of their upright and usually positive implications. Yet this standard technique reduces the need for the reader's intuitive interpretative skills. Furthermore, observing reversals hinders reading the cards' images in visual relation to each other with meaningful cohesiveness. So while reading reversals in this way is a personal choice, this guide will not use them for these reasons. Therefore, turn upright any reversed cards before interpreting them.

Always recall how every card of the deck contains a range of messages from "revealed" to "veiled." Then utilize the following to help determine a card's overall tone in conjunction with your own intuitive sense:

- the card's position in an overall spread
- the card's message in visual relation to other cards present

As already stated, the "veiled" messages are usually hidden from you as pertains to others, situations, and the self in relation to the subject of the particular reading. More subtly, the "veiled" aspects can represent influential factors you have perhaps overlooked, misinterpreted, or are blocking. Sometimes in these cases, awareness of this hidden information is more easily recognized once uncovered. When this occurs, do not consider it a deliberate self-deception. Quite on the contrary, the identification of "veiled" messages—already known on a deeper level—may allow permission to accept such sensitive information on a conscious level for the very first time. Often, this is a significant first step toward desired change. Occultist Nigel Pennick notes, "…we cannot know light without darkness, for total light is as blinding as total darkness. Only through a balance between the opposites can we exist; between light and dark, rigidity and flexibility."[64]

Accepting how messages may indeed be a combination of both "revealed" and "veiled" factors renders the suggested interpretative approach as a genuine challenge. For by it, messages are uncovered by relying upon intuitive awareness while making narrative sense of the visual material found in and between cards. The worthwhile fruit of this inclusive perspective will result in reliable self-readings arising from wiser depths and of genuine practical usefulness. Through them, the gray zones so indicative of much life experiences can be penetrated to achieve a vision beyond the limitations of separateness. In a related way, Hazrat Inayat Khan explains:

> While all things have their opposites, it is also true that in each the spirit of the opposite exists. The closer one approaches reality, the nearer one comes to unity. The evidence of this realization is that no sooner has a question arisen in the heart, than the answer comes as its echo either within or without.[65]

Spreads and Spread Positions

Let us apply the words of the early-20th-century Indian poet Rabindranath Tagore[66] on mystical perception to the core experience of the divination process:

---

64 Nigel Pennick, *The Eldritch World* (Earl Shilton, 2006)

65 Pir Vilayat Inayat Khan, *The Message in Our Time: The Life and Teachings of the Sufi Master Pir-O-Murshid Inayat Khan* (New York, 1979).

66 Rabindranath Tagore was born in 1861 in Kolkata, India where he died in 1941.

There is a point where in the mystery of existence contradictions meet; where movement is not all movement and stillness is not all stillness; where the idea and the form, the within and the without, are united; where infinite becomes finite, yet not losing its infinity.[67]

Some form of guiding map is beneficial while exploring the self-reading's uncharted waters. The spread is just such an instrument. For it provides the framework by which the session's focus is examined or open reading subject defined. The spread is the configuration of the cards upon the reading surface and can incorporate any number of cards and patterns dependent upon the one used. This guide will provide several spreads or layouts comprised of one to six cards that can be adapted for many uses.

A many-faceted interpretation of a particular reading may recognize a variety of meanings and outcomes simultaneously. So then, just begin to consider the multi-layered depths capable of being explored when groupings of only two to four cards are read together as a cohesive unit. A bounty of possibilities ripe for interpretation results! For this very reason, you will find here spreads based in no more than six cards.

Within the larger spread configuration, spread position refers to the placement of an individual card or grouped level of cards typically assigned a particular meaning. Once again, the spread position meanings can be experimented with and altered to suit your purposes. Even so, these meanings should be predetermined beforehand in order to avoid confusion during the actual self-reading process itself.

The spreads to be provided here will focus on *you* as their chief subject. Therefore, view all of the cards' visual elements—human and animal figures, inanimate objects, and otherwise—to primarily represent different aspects of you. Even so and to a lesser degree, sometimes

---

67 Rabindranath Tagore, *Personality* (New York, 1917).

these elements can also indicate aspects of another person directly involved with the particular reading's focus. This is especially so should you identify a figure as such during the reading process. Reflecting our everyday lives, keep in mind how there may be multiple answers to a single question. So then any visual element explored in a card may concurrently indicate aspects of both yourself and another.

Before delving into the individual spreads themselves, let us address the matter of laying the cards into position. As you draw the number of cards required for the spread to be used, place each one facedown into its spread position. Then turn over each one in succession as it is read to build an increasingly detailed picture enriched by growing connections between the cards. While this technique and variations of it are all valid, recommended here is drawing all of the cards needed for the spread following shuffling and cutting. Then lay all the cards face-up before beginning to determine their messages. This allows the opportunity of an initial sweeping overview. During it, ascertain the most crucial aspects of the cards and their connections, as well as the general tone of the self-reading.

Moreover, explore the personal option of the order in which to determine the "revealed" and "veiled" messages, as well as one unifying the two should you feel so inspired. The tiers of the multi-level spreads are designed to explore increasingly numinous realms as they reach progressively higher. So it is recommended to read all of the cards for each tier, starting from the lowest level and then moving higher toward vaster and unified revelation.

Many of the spreads to be explored are followed by sections titled application and connections. The applications offer practical exercises through which greater familiarity with the particular spread can be obtained. The connections sections pose a series of questions to investigate for each spread. Especially in the case of multi-level spreads, their analysis will assist in revealing the illuminating relationships that exist between cards. Several actual sample self-readings have been provided as a way to show the cards and spreads in action. The interpreted messages contained therein present a single exploration not to be considered definitive in any way. In order to more thoroughly grasp the methods provided here, you are strongly encouraged to layout the cards indicated in the sample self-readings as you read through these interpretive sections. Surely, you will uncover interpretations differing, but no less valid than those suggested.

As will be seen, included in some of the spreads are position descriptions that may be spoken aloud during a self-reading. Such a simple and grounding step can assist in imparting even further clarity to the stages of the reading process. Similarly, the spreads' technical explanations are not presented identically purposefully. This will encourage *your own* active and deeper exploration of these pathways toward richly-layered messages.

Each Tarot card offers a range of possible messages to focus upon in a self-reading. Each session allows you to exercise your intuitive awareness. And such awareness will assist in making the interpretive choices from which valuable messages bloom. *This is the unfolding of heart vision.* Your fluency with the spreads will deepen through practice. In order to use effectively the most complex, six-card spreads, comprehension and ease with the perhaps deceptively simpler ones is necessary. So do start with those.[68]

---

68 Typically, Tarot spreads feature a card indicating the subject of the reading. This is unnecessary for the self-reading process explored herein.

Spreads

Assessment
1-card spread
Purpose: To locate and define an imbalance.

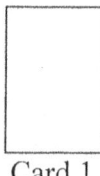
Card 1

The purpose of this spread is to assist in locating and defining an imbalance. Typically, such an imbalance involves, but is not limited to: facing deeper motivations and achieving mystical stages, feeling trapped in harmful situations of a repetitive nature, or managing unconstructive personality aspects. The particular aspect of the imbalance to be explored will best be determined by visual assessment of the card's imagery combined with your intuitive sense—the essential approach for all of the spreads provided herein.

1-Card Spread Application
Begin by specifying an imbalance as the subject of the reading. This can be unfolding in a generalized area, including, but not limited to any one of the following: relationship (familial, friendship, or romantic), career, or along your mystical path.

Part 1
Randomly draw a single card from the already shuffled and cut deck. According to the specified spread position description, define an aspect of the imbalance illustrated by the card as simply as possible.

Spread Position Description

Revealed (Card 1): The known or recently experienced positive aspect of the specified imbalance needing to be embraced.

Part 2

With the same imbalance specified and card used for Part 1 of this application, define an aspect of the imbalance illustrated by the card as simply as possible according to the specified spread position description.

Spread Position Description

Veiled (Card 1): The hidden, overlooked, misinterpreted, or blocked negative aspect of the specified imbalance needing to be embraced or in the process of being released.

Connections

How do the interpretative results from Part 1 and 2 reveal different aspects of the same imbalance?

How do these different aspects influence your present behavior and decision-making processes impacting past and future events?

How do these different aspects assist or hinder you on your their path?

Even if seemingly contradictory, do any similar or overlapping interpretative results exist between the two separate messages?

Synthesize these interpretative results into a unified message providing a fuller understanding of the imbalance.

Imbalance I.D.
2-card spread
Purpose: To define and explore an imbalance.

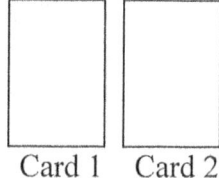

Card 1   Card 2

The purpose of this spread is to define or explore an imbalance in a way more multi-layered than what can be achieved using the 1-card Assessment spread. Once again, such a disparity typically involves, but is not limited to: facing deeper motivations and achieving mystical stages, feeling trapped in harmful situations of a repetitious nature, or managing unconstructive personality aspects. Overall, the focus will be upon a moment when inner realties and outer circumstances are at uncomfortable odds. Although consisting of only two cards, this spread forms the foundation upon which many of the more elaborate ones are constructed.

Spread Position Description

Revealed (Card 1): The known or recently experienced positive aspect of the specified imbalance needing to be embraced.

Veiled (Card 2): The hidden, overlooked, misinterpreted, or blocked negative aspect of the specified imbalance needing to be embraced or in the process of being released.

2-Card Application

Part 1

Using an open reading, randomly draw two cards from the already shuffled and cut deck and place them upon the reading surface in the Imbalance I.D. spread layout. As simply as possible, define the imbalance's two core aspects as illustrated by the cards according to the specified spread position descriptions.

Part 2

Interpret the same two card combination in relation to a specified imbalance unfolding in a generalized area—including, but not limited to relationship (familial, friendship, or romantic), career, or one encountered along your mystical path.

Connections

Explore the following separately for the open reading of Part 1 and the specified reading of Part 2.

How do the messages derived from that which is Revealed (Card 1) and that which is Veiled (Card 2) express different aspects of the same imbalance?

How do these different aspects influence your present behavior and decision-making processes impacting past and future events?

How do these different aspects assist or hinder you on your path?

Even if seemingly contradictory, do any similar or overlapping interpretative results exist between the two separate messages?

If overlapping similarities are interpreted to exist between the two cards, how do they reinforce each other?

If overlapping differences are interpreted to exist between the two cards, how do they intensify the imbalance?

Synthesize these interpretative results into a unified message providing a fuller understanding of the imbalance.

How do the two cards in combination define or explore the imbalance affecting you in a way more fully than what can be achieved using the 1-Card Assessment spread?

Imagine the borders of the two cards dissolving. How might the images' key figures and objects—both animate and inanimate—dialogue with each other, both verbally and through non-verbal action? How might such communication heighten the awareness of each key element? And in this way, how are the original messages expanded and deepened—emotionally, psychologically, and mystically?

Sample Self-Reading

Reading Purpose: The session sought to define the sources of discord in a relationship by asking, "What is the core imbalance causing marital discord?"

Interpretation
Overview

The appearance of two Major Arcana Trumps in a spread consisting of as many cards signaled a particularly potent reading. As such, it was one defined more by motivational forces than individual personalities, realms, or everyday situations—these three represented by the Courts, Aces, and Pips respectively.

Key Aspect
Card 1
The Devil

Considering the reading's exploration of relationship difficulties, the image's enslaved couple is an obvious illustration of the conflict's key aspect. The card may further indicate a shared cycle of destructiveness by the pair's symbolic ties to the Devil's throne. As a Major Arcana card, stressed here is the basic need fueling such repetitive actions as opposed to the actions themselves. This primary need forms the key motivating force causing the conflict. While the card cannot provide the specifics of such a need, the Trump's themes of obsession, control, and conscious dependence describe its type. There was a purposeful focusing on the Trump's veiled aspects considering the reading's difficult topic and the card position's description for this spread. Nevertheless, since the subject of the session entailed two persons, it was important for the reader to concentrate on their own role in this problematic dynamic. Otherwise, there may have been the risk of a time-wasting and ultimately unhelpful shift in focus onto the other party involved—a shift most-often involving the laying on of blame.

Key Opposition or Reinforcement
Card 2
The High Priestess

The solitary and independent nature of the sacred figure depicted is in direct contrast to the Devil's bestial, drone-like underlings. Therefore, this card represents the cause of the core imbalance resulting in the conflict through opposition of the Revealed (Card 1), instead of a reinforcement of it. Since this is a Major Arcana card, the reader attempted to ascertain the key motivating force causing the core imbalance. At her most basic, the High Priestess indicates wisdom obtained through deep reflection and intuitive knowing. The Devil's enchained slaves are transformed into the sanctuary pillars. Between them, the High Priestess sits as mediator of opposites, contemplating endless unseen shades of meaning between light and darkness. The juxtaposition of the two cards side by side provided the reader with a powerful realization of personal responsibility in a detrimental cycle. And with this understanding came the potential of breaking its shackles.

Summary

The reading fulfilled its purpose by assisting in the identification of a troublesome conflict. Obtaining such self-knowledge can be a catalytic process capable of profound change to previous ways of existence. Thus, the conflict affecting the reader had arisen following profound self-reflection resulting in a refusal to repeat a harmful past cycle. A more elaborate spread can offer suggestions as to its resolution. Even so, the reading offered encouragement along the pathway toward hopefully positive change.

Present-Past-Future
3-card spread
Purpose: To identify a Trend Flow.

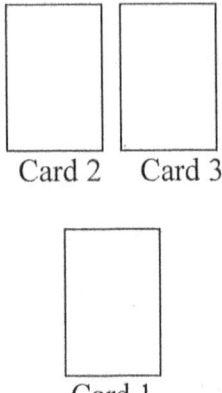

This spread introduces the concept of the Trend Flow; that is, the general direction or most likely outcome of events associated with an imbalance moving across time. These are influenced by a combination of "revealed" and "veiled" aspects. This spread assists in assessing the Trend Flow in your life—its current state, past origins, and future outlook—as well as the way a future challenge may alter its course. Trend Flows may be filled by darkness and light. The recognition and release of the factors contributing to a detrimental one can bring about is resolution. Conversely, those elements identified as fostering a productive Trend Flow should be encouraged and embraced.

What is Happening
Card 1
"This is where I am now."

Spread Position Description: The current Trend Flow in your life.

Major: Your present motivating force contributing to the current Trend Flow.
Court: A personality aspect contributing to the current Trend Flow, or another person causing the same.
Ace: The basic realm manifesting the current Trend Flow.
Pip: The most common situation in which the current Trend Flow occurs.

What Already Possess or Experienced
Card 2
"This is behind me."

Spread Position Description: What you already possess or have experienced contributing to the current Trend Flow.

Major: The past motivating force contributing to the current Trend Flow.
Court: A past personality aspect contributing to the current Trend Flow.
Ace: The basic realm from your past in which the current Trend Flow originated.
Pip: A past experience contributing to the current Trend Flow.

Connections

What are the most significant similarities and differences between What is Happening (Card 1) and What Already Possess or Experienced (Card 2); that is, as relates to the cards' category (Major, Court, Ace, or Pip card) and suit (Wands, Cups, Swords, or Pentacles)?

How do these comparisons reveal the development or static nature of the current Trend Flow across time?

The Challenge
Card 3
"This is before me."

Position Description: A challenge toward change capable of reinforcing and deepening a positive Trend Flow in unexpected ways or breaking the cycle of a negative one.

Major: A motivating force yet unexplored capable of reinforcing and deepening a positive Trend Flow in unexpected ways or breaking the cycle of a negative one.

Court: A yet unexplored personality aspect or a previously uninvolved person capable of reinforcing and deepening a positive Trend Flow in unexpected ways or breaking the cycle of a negative one.

Ace: The basic realm, yet unexplored in which reinforcement and deepening of a positive Trend Flow in unexpected ways can take place, or the breaking of a negative one is possible.

Pip: An uncommon situation capable of reinforcing, deepening, or breaking a Trend Flow.

Connections

What are the most significant similarities and differences between What Already Possess or Experienced (Card 2) and The Challenge (Card 3)—by category (Major, Court, Ace, or Pip card) and suit (Wands, Cups, Swords, or Pentacles)?

How do these comparisons reveal the static or developing nature of the current Trend Flow across time?

Imagine the borders of What Already Possess or Experienced (Card 2) and The Challenge (Card 3) cards dissolving. How might the images' key figures and objects—both animate and inanimate—dialogue with each other, both verbally and through non-verbal action? How might such communication heighten the awareness of each key element? And in this way, how are the original messages expanded and deepened—emotionally, psychologically, and mystically?

Sample Self-Reading

Reading Purpose: The session attempted to explore the basis of a discontented romantic situation while looking toward future possibilities by asking, "In what ways will past experience, current reality, and a potential challenge affect the issue of concern?"

Interpretation
Overview

As one Court card and two Pips were drawn, the reading focused o personality aspects directly affecting happenings in the world. It was notable how none of the three cards fell within the love-related suit of Cups since the reading concerned a similar emotional theme.

What is Happening
Card 1
Queen of Wands

As determined by the spread position, this card describes the present Trend Flow—here, in relation to the reader's romantic life. This position in itself is neither positive nor negative in tone. Therefore, unless a strong indication toward one of them is sensed in advance, the reader should explore a range of both light and dark aspects of the card's meaning when interpreting it. This was the case with the present reading. A Court card drawn here, in combination with the reading purpose, indicates it to be representative of the reader or another romantic party. The reader took the card to represent the self since there was no significant relationship with another at the time of the reading. Hence as defined by the spread position description, the card described personality aspects contributing to the current Trend Flow. The Queen of Wands as lover can be assertive and overtly sexual in a positive manner, but with a tendency toward deviousness and even faithlessness when in a state of imbalance. If the reader is displeased with their love life's current Trend Flow, it is best to examine this Queen's darker leanings and the harm resulting from them. The reader was able to acknowledge an inclination toward self-centeredness and overly demanding behavior if not the object of attention.

What Already Possess or Experienced
Card 2
Six of Swords

During the initial overview, it appeared significant how the cards illustrating the past (Card 2) and future (Card 3) both feature three figures. This might suggest a love dynamic involving more than a traditional couple and the repetition of such a pattern across time. Having already established the reader as an action-oriented Wands monarch (Card 1) helped identify that individual as the decisive figures of the other two cards. Here, the reader as oarsman of the Six of Swords card is responsible for controlling the destinies of the boat's occupants. As defined by the spread's position, the image was interpreted as illustrating a former romantic situation in which the reader was involved simultaneously with more than one person. In the Tarot's symbolic universe, the age of the boat's child passenger may suggest someone simply naïve instead of chronologically young. Keeping in mind this Queen's unsavory characteristics (Card 1), hinted at here is the disloyalty required to maintain such affairs if of a clandestine nature. Alternatively, there may have been an open flaunting of such relationships as a cunning tactic. In particular, this Pip showed the maintenance of a destructive liaison amongst a group. Within the context of the interpretation thus far, the card displayed a past situation devised by the reader producing a harmful trend. Moreover, while its immediate gains seemed appealing at the time, the reader's displeasure at the then current situation and future concerns about it revealed a desire for change.

The Challenge
Card 3
Five of Swords

As mentioned already, the reader perceived parallels between the three-figured scenes depicting past (Card 2) and future (Card 3) situations. Considering the reader's disappointment, the function of this spread position proposed a challenge capable of breaking the negative cycle. Since a Pip, it showed a situation uncommon to the reader with the power to achieve this end. The interpretation of the scene was one of comeuppance not initially comprehended by the temporarily victorious reader. Lost in self-satisfaction, the sword-hording central figure does not realize the other two have abandoned the situation upon realizing the duplicity used against them. This reading of the card does not make a definite prediction of such a happening actually occurring. Instead, the reader interpreted the image as the potential results from current modes of existence. The reader contemplated the use of previously untried approaches in romance of a less controlling nature. The inherent vulnerability of such modes would prove challenging for the reader—but a risk felt worth taking for more satisfactory relationships.

Summary

The session proved understandably daunting in parts for the reader with its mostly somber analysis of a sensitive topic. When delving into such turbulent waters, maintain focus upon the more positive attributes attached to your representatives in the cards—here, the Queen of Wands' (Card 1) ability to pursue her desires; the oarsman's perseverance from the Six of Swords (Card 2); and even the victor's cleverness, when used constructively, as seen in the Five of Swords (Card 3). While different forms of love appear in all suits of the Tarot, the Cups hold the fullest expression of the romantic variety of interest to this particular reading. Their absence among the cards drawn stress what was possibly lacking in the reader's approach to matters of the heart. Sometimes the cards' most potent advice resides in the ones conspicuously missing in relation to the reading's purpose. Using this observation as a starting point, the reader felt encouraged to consider the disparity between the romantic goals hoped for and the apparently counterproductive methods used to obtain them.

While being conducted, the reader did not experience the atmosphere of the session as one of self-accusation or condemnation. Be wary of harshly judging yourself. Strive to receive the cards' messages with utmost honesty and enthusiasm toward desired transformation. Know how interpretations are never definitive or unable to be further deepened. The latter takes place with the wisdom gained through the self-reading practice and the actual experience of living.

Trend Flow
4-card spread
Purpose: To further explore a Trend Flow more deeply.

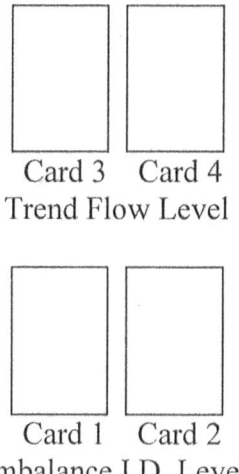

Card 3 Card 4
Trend Flow Level

Card 1 Card 2
Imbalance I.D. Level

This spread builds progressively upon those previously explored. Its purpose is to delve deeper still into the concept of the Trend Flow; this being the general direction or most likely outcome of events associated with an imbalance moving forward across time. The spread's first level focuses on identifying an imbalance experienced at the time of the reading.

The direction of the Trend Flow's movement can be determined by comparing the cards representing it (Cards 3 and 4) with those defining other time-related aspects—for this spread, those indicating the present imbalance (Cards 1 and 2). Depending on the reading's focus, the Trend Flow for this spread can be adjusted as well to describe the past source of the present imbalance. As already noted, such an approach accepts a dynamic interaction between past, present, and potential realities to arrive at multi-dimensional messages.

Imbalance I.D. Level
Spread Position Description

Revealed (Card 1): The known or presently experienced positive aspect of the specified imbalance needing to be embraced.

Veiled (Card 2): The hidden, overlooked, misinterpreted, or blocked negative presently experienced aspect of the specified imbalance needing to be embraced or in the process of being released.

Trend Flow Level
Spread Position Description

Revealed (Card 3): The to-be-known or experienced positive transformation of the imbalance if the message of Card 1 is embraced.

Veiled (Card 4): The to-be-known or experienced negative transformation of the imbalance if the message of Card 2 is rejected.

4-Card Application

Using either a reading focusing on a specific issue or an open one, identify the current state of an imbalance and its Trend Flow affecting you. This application will utilize the Trend Flow level to indicate moving forward across time.

Connections

Before exploring the following inquiries, apply the Connections section for the Imbalance I.D. to Cards 1 and 2 of this application.

What are the most significant similarities and differences between the present imbalance (Cards 1 and 2) and the Trend Flow (Cards 3 and 4 as transformed from Cards 1 and 2)?

Determine a unified message for the Imbalance I.D. level (Cards 1 and 2) and the Trend Flow level (Cards 3 and 4). Do these overall messages indicate a positive or negative transformation?

How do these comparisons reveal the evolving or stagnating movement of the Trend Flow forward across time?

Imagine the borders of the Imbalance I.D. (Cards 1 and 2) dissolving. How might the images' key figures and objects—both animate and inanimate—dialogue with each other, both verbally and through non-verbal action? How might such communication heighten the awareness of each key element? And in this way, how are the original messages expanded and deepened—emotionally, psychologically, and mystically? Now do the same for the Trend Flow (Cards 3 and 4).

What similarities and differences exist between Cards 1 and 3? What do they confirm about the "revealed" aspects of the reading's focus?

What similarities and differences exist between Cards 2 and 4? What do they confirm about the "revealed" aspects of the reading's focus?

Imagine the borders of Cards 1 and 3 cards dissolving. How might the images' key figures and objects—both animate and inanimate—dialogue with each other, both verbally and through non-verbal action? How might such communication heighten the awareness of each key element? And in this way, how are the original messages expanded and deepened—emotionally, psychologically, and mystically? Now do the same for Cards 2 and 4.

Remove Cards 2 and 3. Align remaining Cards 1 and 4 into a single, horizontal row—Card 1 to the left of Card 4. Abandon the spread position descriptions used prior to view what were the reading's original starting and ending points (Cards 1 and 4) as an evolving journey.

Compare, contrast, and synthesize their messages to determine the overall sweep of the reading from this alternate and further distilled perspective.

Imagine the borders of the two cards dissolving on each level. How might the images' key figures and objects—both animate and inanimate—dialogue with each other on the different levels, both verbally and through non-verbal action? Further envision the same process between the two levels; that is, Card 1 in dialogue with Card 3, and Card 2 with Card 4. Explore diagonal dialogues between Cards 1 and 4, and Cards 2 and 3. As this is done, be sure to consider the message of each level. How might such communication heighten the awareness of each key element? And in this way, how are the original messages expanded and deepened—emotionally, psychologically, and mystically?

Crossroads
5-card spread
Purpose: To assist on a "yes or no" decision.

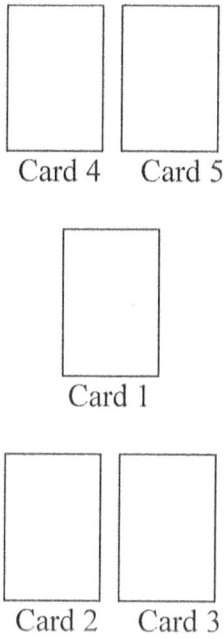

Anthropologist, psychologist and author, Nicholaj de Mattos Frisvold notes, "It is to the crossroads we go to make decisions. It is at the crossroads we set the course for the journey. It is at the crossroads we confront ourselves and realize our power."[69] This spread is useful for assessing the positive (revealed) and negative (veiled) aspects existing in both options of an impending "yes or no" decision. The choice ultimately belongs to you. Because of its analytical use for a particular issue, this spread is not recommended for what has been described

---

69   Nicholaj de Mattos Frisvold, *Craft of the Untamed: An inspired vision of Traditional Witchcraft* (Oxford, 2011)

previously here as an open reading. This spread will introduce the use of card positions with specific positive or negative connotations to describe the same issue. As a result, experience with it will emphasize the dualistic nature of most everyday decisions and stress a reading's inability to provide overly simplistic answers to them. In addition to their more typical uses explored in earlier spreads here, this one will familiarize you with perceiving Court cards as describers of types of actions, as well as moods surrounding a situation.

The Decision
Card 1
"This is my decision."

Spread Position Description: The impending decision affecting you.

Major: The key motivating force involved in the decision.

Court: The key personality aspect involved in the decision, or another key person involved in the decision-making process. Or, how to describe the mood surrounding the decision, or the way the decision may be typified.

Ace: The key realm manifesting the decision.

Pip: The key situation in which the decision is to occur.

No/Pro
Card 2
"This is the positive in deciding against it."

Spread Position Description: The potentially positive aspect in deciding against it.

Major: The key motivating force affected positively by a decision against it.

Court: The key personality aspect improved by a decision against it, or another key person affected positively by your decision against it. Or, how to describe the positive mood surrounding the decision against, or the positive way the decision against it may be typified.

Ace: The key realm affected positively by a decision against it.

Pip: The key situation improved by a decision against it.

No/Con
Card 3
"This is the negative in deciding against it."

Position Description: The potentially negative aspect in deciding against it.

Major: The key motivating force affected negatively by a decision against it.

Court: The key personality aspect contributing to a decision against it, or another key person influencing your decision against it. Or, how to describe the negative mood surrounding the decision against it, or the negative way the decision against it may be typified.

Ace: The key realm affected negatively by a decision against it.

Pip: The key situation impaired by a decision against it.

Connections

Are No/Pro (Card 2) and No/Con (Card 3) of the same or different category (Major, Court, Ace, or Pip card), suit (Wands, Cups, Swords, or Pentacles), or rank if a Court card (King, Queen, Knight, or Page)? Do the positive aspects of No/Pro (Card 2) outweigh that of No/Con (Card 3) or vice versa?

In what ways are these two cards similar and different from each other?

Yes/Pro
Card 4
"This is the positive in deciding for it."

Position Description: The potentially positive aspect in deciding for it.

Major: The key motivating force affected positively by a decision for it.

Court: The key personality aspect improved by a decision for it, or another key person affected positively by your decision for it. Or, how to describe the positive mood surrounding the decision for it, or the positive way the decision for it may be typified.

Ace: The key realm affected positively by a decision for it.

Pip: The key situation improved by a decision for it.

Connections

Are No/Pro (Card 2) and Yes/Pro (Card 4) of the same or different category (Major, Court, Ace, or Pip card), suit (Wands, Cups, Swords, or Pentacles), or rank if a Court card (King, Queen, Knight, or Page)? Do the positive aspects of No/Pro (Card 2) outweigh that of Yes/Pro (Card 4) or vice versa? In what ways are these two cards similar and different from each other?

Yes/Con
Card 5
"This is the negative in deciding for it."

Position Description: The potentially negative aspect in deciding for it.

Major: The key motivating force affected negatively by a decision for it.

Court: The key personality aspect impaired by a decision for it, or another key person affected negatively by your decision for it. Or, how to describe the negative mood surrounding the decision for it, or the negative way the decision for it may be typified.

Ace: The key realm affected negatively by a decision for it.

Pip: The key situation impaired by a decision for it.

Connections

Are Yes/Pro (Card 4) and Yes/Con (Card 5) of the same or different category (Major, Court, Ace, or Pip card), suit (Wands, Cups, Swords, or Pentacles), or rank if a Court card (King, Queen, Knight, or Page)? Does the negativity of No/Con (Card 3) outweigh that of Yes/Con (Card 5) or vice versa?

In what ways are these two cards similar and different from each other?

Imagine the borders of No/Pro (Card 2) and No/Con (Card 3) dissolving. How might the images' key figures and objects—both animate and inanimate—dialogue with each other, both verbally and through non-verbal action? How might such communication heighten the awareness of each key element? And in this way, how are the original messages expanded and deepened—emotionally, psychologically, and mystically? Now do the same for Yes/Pro (Card 4) and Yes/Con (Card 5).

Note: For a more in-depth session, you may choose to return to Cards 2 through 5 in order to analyze them in terms of their opposite connotations as determined by their individual spread positions. So for example, reinterpret No/Pro (Card 2), or the potentially positive aspect in deciding against it, to include its potentially negative connotations as well. Once again, such a revaluation will stress the dualistic nature of decisions.

Sample Self-Reading

Reading Purpose: In moving forward with a new business venture by asking, "What are the positive and negative aspects of this decision?"

Interpretation
Overview

The Major and Minor Arcana cards drawn for the reading concerned opposing issues of harnessing and relinquishing control, as well as those involving independent and joined forces. All of these issues were of crucial relevance to a reader about to embark on an important enterprise.

The Decision
Card 1
Eight of Cups

In the scope of the spread, the purpose of this position is to define the nature of the impending decision affecting the reader. Drawing a Pip card here helped identify the key situation surrounding the decision. The trekker pictured in the Eight of Cups represented the reader starting on a new quest. That the figure is setting off alone during a time of darkness indicates the genuine perils involved in its undertaking—even if the eclipse as depicted symbolizes the temporariness of this condition. Furthermore, the reader extended the scene's interpretation to include others' negative perception of the undertaking as well. With the series of abandoned upright cups symbolizing considerable assets already possessed, the reader's detractors may have perceived the enterprise as foolhardy and wasteful. The suit of Cups suggests these goods as being of an emotional, non-monetary value. So perhaps the critics were fearful of losing the reader's attentions as a byproduct of the energy and time-consuming demands of the pending endeavor. Regardless, the solitary nature of the Pip figure's expedition affirmed the reader's single-minded determination to undertake the decision.

No/Pro
Card 2
The Empress

For this particular reading, a Major Arcana card here stood for the reader's key motivating force potentially affected positively by a decision to halt the business venture. In the role of loving Empress, the reader would continue to bestow the bounty indicated in the previous Pip (Card 1) with characteristic generosity. Nevertheless, such giving would only be possible at the sake of abandoning the business aspirations fueling the venture. Of course and as noted earlier, this might please those desiring the reader to surrender the plan under consideration. However, even though this spread position's purpose is to examine positive aspects, the reader detected darker ones as well. Most notably, the makings of discontented complacency by an ever-lounging monarch (Card 2) in comparison with the risk-taking journeyman (Card 1) made the latter figure that much more admirable to the reader.

No/Con
Card 3
Nine of Swords

While the previous spread positions were inherently neutral (Card 1) or positive (Card 2) in tone, the nature of this one stresses the darker qualities of the particular card drawn. Here, a Pip would demonstrate the key situation manifesting such negativity. Therefore, the Nine of Swords illustrated this potentially harmful aspect should the business venture not take place. Immediately, the reader identified with the tormented figure of the scene. Choosing whether to make this significant life event had already consumed innumerable sleepless nights, with more sure to follow. The reader explained how, separate from the decision definer (Card 1), the remaining cards (Cards 2-5) spoke of future prospects. This understanding expanded the reader's original perception of the Pip in question. In the context of the reading, then, the anxiety experienced by the figure shifted to represent the reader's possible regret if the business plan under consideration never came to fruition. The reader compared the lighter (Card 2) and darker (Card 3) aspects of the same negative decision. Combining the implications of both of these cards, the reader contemplated how the benevolent sovereign (Card 2) exemplified the daytime façade of the same figure whose endless nights were a misery (Card 3).

Yes/Pro
Card 4
The Chariot

A Major Arcana card in this spread position describes the key motivating force affected positively in a decision for the issue at hand. As such, the charioteer illustrated the reader's resultant sense of command should the business venture be made real. It was interesting to note how Major Arcana cards appeared to express the optimistic effects of both a choice against (Card 2) or in support (Card 4) of the decision. This implied a deeper manifestation of these same effects as opposed to those felt through everyday situations. The Pips drawn for two other spread positions (Cards 3 and 5) illustrated such situational outcomes. The reader deemed the mastery exhibited by the charioteer the most appealing of the possibilities presented thus far in the session.

Yes/Con
Card 5
Two of Cups

The function of this spread position is to show the potentially negative aspect of making a positive decision. In light of the reading purpose, the negative aspects of the Pip drawn represented the key situation impaired by realizing the business venture. Most pertinent among the darker features of the Two of Cups centered on unproductive partnerships. Furthermore, the suit itself implied the origins of such a union in an emotional arena largely unrelated to commerce. Consequently, the interpretation included the possible hazards of the reader joining forces in the enterprise with a family member, spouse, or romantic companion; or perhaps the damaging of a key emotion-based relationship should the business venture move forward. Also explored was the less obvious symbolism of the Pip's couple as representing the reader's internal-conflicts about the project. Obviously, these concerns would continue even if the venture was undertaken. The next portion of the interpretation compared the negativity expressed by the cards should the reader not proceed with the enterprise (Card 3) or if it was indeed pursued (Card 5). The reader felt the risks expressed in the Two of Cups (Card 5) preferable to the profound remorse represented by the inaction indicated by the Nine of Swords (Card 3) in this reading.

Summary

Although aware of their presence, the reader began the session with an unclear sense of the problematic issues surrounding the business venture. The cards provided an objective perspective of these apprehensions and more by depicting the potential benefits of this life-altering decision as well. The reader especially appreciated the attention drawn to the dangers of converting a personal liaison into a business partnership since it was an option then under definite consideration. As a result, the session helped clarify the conflicts surrounding this important milestone on the reader's journey by offering an objective path on which to advance.

Arch Bridge
5-card spread
Purpose: To resolve a conflict.

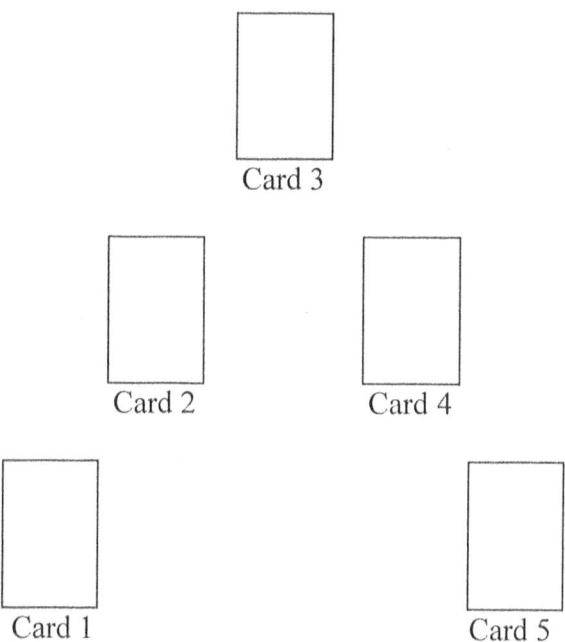

Adapt this 5-card spread for a variety of conflict resolution purposes. The layout visually follows the curve of an arch bridge, one of the most ancient forms of bridge building. The inherent solidity of such a structure is the result of simple, yet highly effective design. By it, there is a distribution of the bridge's overall weight along its curve down to the supports located at either end. Positioned at the center of the arch, the keystone prevents the bridge from collapsing entirely. As such, it is the structure's single most important element. The general meanings of the following spread positions reflect several of these architectural concepts symbolically. Read the cards in clockwise numerical order as indicated to take the journey over the arch bridge.

Foundation
Card 1

Spread Position Description: The reality of the issue affecting you, such as a motivating force (Major Arcana), a personality aspect (Court), realm (Ace), or situation (Pip).

Building Block
Card 2

Spread Position Description: What is essential or should be encouraged in order for you to reach the desired outcome. This includes a helpful motivating force (Major Arcana), a particular aspect of your personality (Court), realm (Ace), or constructive situation (Pip).

Keystone
Card 3

Spread Position Description: What you need to understand more deeply or accept more fully yielding the most successful resolution of the issue or conflict. This may be your motivating force (Major Arcana) or personality aspect (Court), realm (Ace), or situation (Pip).

Connections

How do the requirements of the Keystone (Card 3) confirm the messages of the Building Block (Card 2)?

Weak Point
Card 4

Position Description: That which should be released since it is either unsound or in excess of what is needed to reach the desired outcome, such as a destructive motivating force (Major Arcana) or personality aspect (Court), realm (Ace), or repetitious situation (Pip).

Connections

In what ways are the Building Block (Card 2) and the Weak Point (Card 4) similar and different from each other?

Other Side
Card 5

Position Description: The hoped-for outcome of the issue or conflict possible through its resolution, along with unanticipated benefits. This includes a beneficial motivating force (Major Arcana), personality aspect (Court), realm (Ace), or situation (Pip).

Connections

In what ways are the Foundation (Card 1) and the Other Side (Card 5) similar and different from each other?

Imagine the borders of the Foundation (Card 1) and the Building Block (Card 2) dissolving. How might the images' key figures and objects—both animate and inanimate—dialogue with each other, both verbally and through non-verbal action? How might such communication heighten the awareness of each key element? And in this way, how are the original messages expanded and deepened—emotionally, psychologically, and mystically? Now progressively, do the same for the Building Block (Card 2) and the Keystone (Card 3), the Keystone (Card 3) and the Weak Point (Card 4), and then the Weak Point (Card 4) and the Other Side (Card 5). And finally, view the entire arch of cards as a seamless procession of figures and elements sharing the same space.

Let this become one of the centuries' old processional *trionfi* parades of Italy described earlier. How does such an all-encompassing perspective expand your understanding of the reading's messages?

Guidance
6-card spread
Purpose: To offer guidance for a variety of situations.

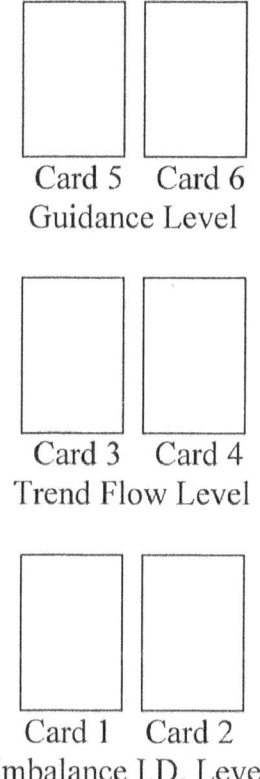

Card 5   Card 6
Guidance Level

Card 3   Card 4
Trend Flow Level

Card 1   Card 2
Imbalance I.D. Level

Building upon the Trend Flow spread, the purpose of this one is to offer you valuable guidance. Issuing from a higher source, the insight pouring from the topmost level (Cards 5 and 6) will illuminate all levels ascending to its heights. The wisdom accessed here will assist you to rise to this summit—most notably through the transformative challenges existing between the Imbalance I.D. level (Cards 1 and 2) and the Trend Flow level (Cards 3 and 4). This inspired information ranges from shifts in perspective to untried modes of behavior producing the maximum benefit.

Imbalance I.D. Level
Spread Position Description

Revealed (Card 1): The known or presently experienced positive aspect of the specified imbalance needing to be embraced.

Veiled (Card 2): The hidden, overlooked, misinterpreted, or blocked presently experienced negative aspect of the specified imbalance needing to be embraced or in the process of being released.

Trend Flow Level
Spread Position Description

Revealed (Card 3): The to-be-known or experienced positive transformation of the imbalance if the message of Card 1 is embraced.

Veiled (Card 4): The to-be-known or experienced negative transformation of the imbalance if the message of Card 2 is rejected.

Guidance Level
Spread Position Description

Revealed (Card 5): A light-filled, positive perspective shift or behavior mode to be adopted in relation to the imbalance and elsewhere.

Veiled (Card 6): A hidden, or overlooked, misinterpreted, or blocked perspective or mode of behavior fostering the imbalance needing to be embraced and released.

6-Card Spread Application

Using either a reading focusing on a specific issue or an open one, identify the current state of an imbalance (Cards 1 and 2) and its Trend

Flow (Cards 1 and 2 transformed into Cards 3 and 4) affecting you. Then, determine the guidance (Cards 5 and 6) most helpful to you in managing the Trend Flow.

Connections

Before proceeding, apply all except the last of the inquiries found in this Connections section for the Trend Flow to Cards 1 through 4 of this application.

Imagine the borders of the Guidance level (Cards 5 and 6) dissolving. How might the images' key figures and objects—both animate and inanimate—dialogue with each other, both verbally and through non-verbal action? How might such communication heighten the awareness of each key element? And in this way, how are the original messages expanded and deepened—emotionally, psychologically, and mystically?

How does the guidance message (Cards 5 and 6) compare and contrast with the identified imbalance (Cards 1 and 2) and the Trend Flow (Cards 3 and 4 as transformed from Cards 1 and 2)?

Shape the guidance message into a challenge shaped to assist you to meet the transformative challenges existing between the Imbalance I.D. level (Cards 1 and 2) and the Trend Flow level (Cards 3 and 4).

View the starting and ending points (Cards 1 and 6) as a journey. By comparing and contrasting them, determine the overall sweep of the reading's central message.

Remove Cards 2 through 5. Align remaining Cards 1 and 6 into a single, horizontal row—Card 1 to the left of Card 6. Abandon the spread position descriptions used prior to view what were the reading's original starting and ending points (Cards 1 and 6) as an evolving journey.

Compare, contrast, and synthesize their messages to determine the overall sweep of the reading from this different and further distilled perspective.

Extend the border dissolution process between all three levels; that is, let Card 1 dialogue with Card 3, Card 2 with Card 4, Card 3 with Card 5, and Card 4 with Card 6. Explore diagonal dialogues as described earlier in the Trend Flow spread: Trend Flow, with additional conversational opportunities provided by the third level of the present spread. Experiment with jumping over levels—let dialogues happen between Card 1 and Card 5, Card 2 and Card 6, or any combination thereof. As this is done, be sure to consider the message revealed at each level. How might such communication heighten the awareness of each key element? And in this way, how are the original messages expanded and deepened—emotionally, psychologically, and mystically?

Prepared Deck Application
Major and Minor Arcana Connection

This application requires a specially prepared deck. Use it with even-numbered spreads constructed of side-by-side levels consisting of two cards each. This includes: Imbalance I.D., Trend Flow, and Guidance spreads.

To gain familiarity with this application, use it with the Guidance spread for either a reading focusing on a specific issue or an open one to identify the current state of an imbalance (Cards 1 and 2) and its Trend Flow (Cards 1 and 2 transformed into Cards 3 and 4) affecting you. Then determine the guidance (Cards 5 and 6) most helpful in managing the Trend Flow.

To prepare, begin by separating the entire deck between the Major and Minor Arcana cards. Place the two piles picture-facedown upon the center of the reading surface. Then shuffle each pile in any preferred standard or non-standard method. Concentrate on the reading's intention during this action. In the case of an open reading, simply calm the mind, assisted by a few full breaths, to promote a receptive state. Keeping each pile separate, thoroughly mix the cards before gathering them back together, all the while maintaining their facedown position.

Draw three cards one by one from the Major Arcana pile, placing them in the spread positions for Cards 1, 3, and 5 starting from the lowest position (Card 1). Then draw three cards from the Minor Arcana pile, placing these alongside in spread positions for Cards 2, 4, and 6, again starting from the lowest position (Card 2).

During the reading process, analyze each of the 2-card combination levels, making special note as to how the Major Arcana messages (Cards 1, 3, and 5) directly illuminate those of the Minor Arcana (Cards 2, 4, and 6) by specifying their deeper, "unseen" source.

Adding Depth through the Shadow Level

The occultist and artist Austin Osman Spare[70] states, "It was the straying that found the path direct."[71] In that adventurous spirit, you are encouraged to experiment with enlarging any of the previously-described spreads by adding additional levels. For example, for a more in-depth reading, add a further level dedicated to important aspects from the past. As already noted, the Trend Flow level of the Trend Flow spread can be adjusted to focus on previously experienced sources of present imbalances. This is done by dedicating the Trend Flow level to forward-

---

70 Austin Osman Spare was born in London in 1886 where he died in 1956. In 2013, a hand-painted, seventy-eight card Tarot deck created by the artist c. 1906 was discovered. Learn more in the following book: Jonathan Allen, ed. *Lost Envoy: The Tarot Deck of Austin Osman Spare* (London, 2016).

71 Austin Osman Spare, *The Writings of Austin Osman Spare: Anathema of Zos, The Book of Pleasure, and The Focus of Life* (Sioux Falls, 2010).

moving transformational changes, while adding a new two-card level in between the Imbalance I.D. level and the Trend Flow level for important indicators of the past.

A Shadow level can be adopted as appropriate. Here, the Shadow represents influential factors you are potentially unaware of, have overlooked, or are blocking. Sometimes, you may recognize these hidden aspects once uncovered. When this occurs, do not consider it an instance of deliberate self-delusion. On the contrary, the identification of the Shadow in the reading may allow you permission to accept such sensitive information openly at last. Obviously, because of its intense nature, undertake Shadow level exploration with discretion and utmost care.

Devise new levels to add additional meaning to any of the spreads. Once again, assigning the message of a particular spread position or level should be established always before you draw the cards for the reading. As a further challenge, reduce each level of any spread featuring multiple levels constructed of more than one card to the single card of it which speaks most directly to the reading at hand. Then by its "revealed" and "veiled" aspects, determine a unified message for that level. Apply this refining process to the following spreads: Trend Flow, Crossroads, and Guidance spreads; as well as the subsequent Heart of the Matter and Soul of the Matter spreads.

Heart of the Matter
6-card spread
Purpose: To identify and resolve a variety of conflicts.

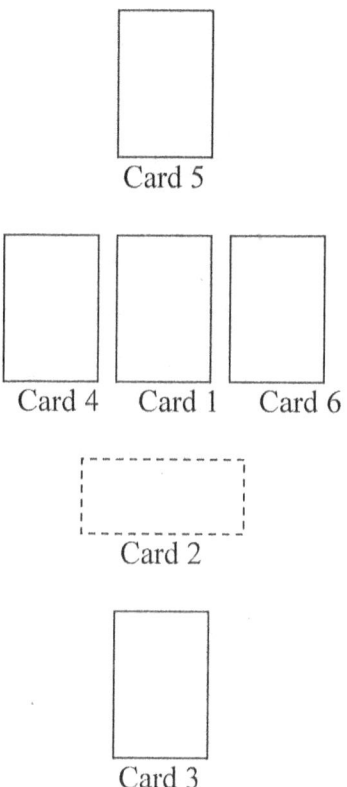

This spread is beneficial in identifying a conflict experienced by the reader, fostering awareness of a resultant Trend Flow, and then describing a challenge toward its resolution. This spread incorporates the previously introduced Shadow concept. And while not predicting definite future events, here the expanded message of the Trend Flow

(Card 5) suggests a more likely outcome than in the Present-Past-Future spread.

Place Card 2 horizontally across Card 1 during the initial laying out of the cards. Then turn Card 2 upright to the right-hand side of Card 1 during the reading process. Determine additional messages by completing this assessment with Card 2 placed to the left-hand side of Card 1.

Key Aspect
Card 1
"This I know."

Spread Position Description: The known key aspect of the conflict.
Major: The known key motivating force causing the conflict.
Court: The known key personality aspect causing the conflict, or another known key person causing the same.
Ace: The known key realm manifesting the conflict.
Pip: The known key situation in which the conflict occurs.

Key Opposition or Reinforcement
Card 2
"This crosses or supports me."

Spread Position Description: The known cause of the core imbalance of the conflict through opposition or reinforcement of the Key Aspect (Card 1).

Major: The known key motivating force in either yourself or another person causing the core imbalance of the conflict through opposition or reinforcement of the Key Aspect (Card 1).

Court: The known key personality aspect of yourself, or the known key person causing the core imbalance of the conflict through opposition or reinforcement of the Key Aspect (Card 1).

Ace: The known key realm causing the core imbalance of the

conflict through opposition or reinforcement of the Key Aspect (Card 1).

Pip: The known key situation causing the core imbalance of the conflict through opposition or reinforcement of the Key Aspect (Card 1).

Connections

Are the Key Aspect (Card 1) and Key Opposition or Reinforcement (Card 2) of the same or different category (Major, Court, Ace, or Pip card), suit (Wands, Cups, Swords, or Pentacles), or rank if a Court card (King, Queen, Knight, or Page)?

In what ways do these cards oppose or reinforce each other?

How does the Key Aspect (Card 1) and the Key Opposition or Reinforcement (Card 2) help identify each other?

Shadow
Card 3
"This is what is hidden."

Spread Position Description: The Shadow aspect contributing to the conflict you are unaware of, have overlooked, or may be blocking.

Major: The motivating Shadow aspect contributing to the conflict you are unaware of, have overlooked, or may be blocking.

Court: The Shadow personality aspect contributing to the conflict you are unaware of, have overlooked, or may be blocking; or, another person contributing the same who you are unaware of, have overlooked, or of whose involvement you may be blocking awareness.

Ace: The basic Shadow realm affecting the conflict you are unaware of, have overlooked, or you may be blocking awareness.

Pip: The Shadow situation manifesting the conflict the reader may be unaware of, have overlooked, or may be blocking.

Connections

What does the Shadow (Card 3) reveal about the hidden nature of the Key Aspect (Card 1) and Key Opposition or Reinforcement (Card 2)? Does the Shadow (Card 3) reinforce or oppose either the Key Aspect (Card 1) or the Key Opposition or Reinforcement (Card 2) more strongly than the other?

What Already Possess or Experienced
Card 4
"This is behind me."

Spread Position Description: What you already possess or have experienced contributing to the conflict.

Major: The past motivating force contributing to the conflict.
Court: The past aspect of your personality contributing to the conflict.
Ace: The basic realm from your past in which the conflict originated.
Pip: A past experience contributing to the conflict.

Connections

Does any aspect of What Already Possess or Experienced (Card 4) help clarify the source of the conflict as identified by the Key Aspect (Card 1)?

Trend Flow
Card 5
"This may crown me."

Spread Position Description: The probable outcome of the conflict consistent with its aspects as detailed in Cards 1-4.

Major: The main motivating force characterizing the most likely outcome of the conflict.

Court: The aspect of your personality characterizing the most likely outcome of the conflict, or another person doing the same. Or, how the mood surrounding the most likely outcome of the conflict can be described, or the way it may be typified.

Ace: The basic realm manifesting the most likely outcome of the conflict.

Pip: The situation characterizing the most likely outcome of the conflict.

Connections

Are What Already Possess or Experienced (Card 4) and the Trend Flow (Card 5) of the same or different category (Major, Court, Ace, or Pip card) or suit (Wands, Cups, Swords, or Pentacles)?

Does the comparison of these two cards indicate a continuation of a past cycle, a change to it, or the development of a new one?

The Challenge
Card 6
"This is before me."

Spread Position Description: A challenge toward change capable of altering the conflict or Trend Flow.

Major: A motivating force yet unexplored capable of altering the conflict or Trend Flow

Court: A yet unexplored aspect of your personality capable of altering the conflict or Trend Flow; or, a previously uninvolved person who may do the same.

Ace: The basic realm, yet unexplored, in which alteration of the conflict or Trend Flow is possible.

Pip: An uncommon situation that is capable of altering the conflict or Trend Flow.

Connections

Are the Trend Flow (Card 5) and The Challenge (Card 6) of the same or different category (Major, Court, Ace, or Pip card), suit (Wands, Cups, Swords, or Pentacles), or rank if a Court card (King, Queen, Knight, or Page)?

How does risk of accepting The Challenge (Card 6) compare with the resolution of the conflict, as identified by the Key Aspect (Card 1) and the Key Opposition or Reinforcement (Card 2), or continuation of the Trend Flow (Card 5)?

Imagine the borders of Cards 4, 1 and 6 dissolving. How might the images' key figures and objects—both animate and inanimate—dialogue with each other, both verbally and through non-verbal action? How might such communication heighten the awareness of each key element? And in this way, how are the original messages expanded and deepened—emotionally, psychologically, and mystically? And finally, view the borders of this trio of cards dissolving to make a seamless procession of figures and elements sharing the same space. How does such an all-encompassing perspective expand your understanding of the reading's messages?

Sample Self-Reading
Reading Purpose: an open reading

Interpretation
Overview

The appearance of both Major and Minor Arcana cards centered on mental or psychological upset in contrast to others representing advanced modes of integration signaled an interior disturbance of potentially harmful proportions. When an open reading is decided upon, as it was in this case, an interpretation was built carefully by surveying all aspects of the cards and their interrelationships in order to ascertain areas of conflict.

Key Aspect
Card 1
The Moon

The first two cards of this spread function in the same manner as the previously examined Imbalance I.D. spread. However, this more detailed spread includes the Shadow (Card 3) in order to differentiate between known from unknown aspects of the conflict. A Major Arcana card in this spread position outlines the known key motivating force causing the conflict. The darker elements of The Moon would suggest this to encompass self-doubt and an inability to confront an uncomfortable truth. While the same Trump is often associated with deeply meditative processes beneath consciousness, this spread position is concerned with those the reader was aware of to a much more easily accessed degree.

Key Opposition or Reinforcement
Card 2
Three of Swords

The intellectual realm of Swords complements the contemplative nature of The Moon (Card 1). Therefore, the particular Pip drawn illustrated the known key situation causing the core imbalance of the conflict through reinforcement of the Trump (Card 1). The suit indicated such a situation as one possibly marked by difficulties in communication and decision-making. More specifically, the reader perceived the Three of

Swords as representing the outcome of an enduring mental wound. This injury manifested itself in ways known and as such became a cause for concern.

Shadow
Card 3
The Magician

A Major Arcana card drawn for this spread position uncovers the motivating Shadow aspect contributing to the conflict. The Magician's positive attributes of charisma and skillful competence contrast directly with the stagnating negative aspects of The Moon (Card 1) and the Three of Swords (Card 2). Ironically, the obviousness of such a blatant difference is often a signal of an issue the reader is unaware of, has overlooked, or may be blocking in the self. The evolving interpretation proposed how the key conflict (Cards 1 and 2) had obstructed the reader's progress symbolized by The Magician (Card 3). So then, the resultant frustration acted as a hidden motivator (Card 3) by causing the reader to realize an issue was in need of resolution—perhaps even encouraging the reading experience itself.

What Already Possess or Experienced
Card 4
Seven of Pentacles

In addition to describing the reader's past experience contributing to the conflict, this card's secondary function is to further identify the source of the Key Aspect (Card 1). The Seven of Pentacles addresses concerns ranging from the necessity of patience to errors due to impulsiveness. Hence, the interpretation of this card viewed it as representing previous situations marked by poor timing. Additionally, the reader perceived how this Pip sometimes symbolizes the negative act of reaping the benefits from others' efforts. Note was made of the suit's relevant realm of practical situations and the previous cards' issues of mental or psychological upset (Card 2) and blocked adeptness (Card 3). These factors together formed the foundation of the conflict and described those areas in which it affected the reader's current everyday life.

Trend Flow
Card 5
The Devil

A Major Arcana card in this spread position indicates the reader's main motivating force characterizing the conflict's most likely outcome. The Devil's affirmative power issues from a passionate drive capable of overcoming obstacles. When misdirected or needlessly wasted, this same force leads the individual away from worthy goals to settle for what is easiest. Accordingly, this Trump amplified the discouragement already illustrated by the subjects of The Magician (Card 3) and the Seven of Pentacles (Card 4). The similar theme of stagnancy evident in both the past (Card 4) and the Trend Flow (Card 5) showed the continuation of a harmful cycle. The Devil's submissively chained minions offered a clue as to the cause of the Trend Flow. If seen as representing the reader alone, the pair then represented an essential split at the basis of the conflict. Most notably, this division took place between self-doubt (Cards 1 and 2) and taking competent action (Card 3) resulting in delayed responsiveness or recklessness (Card 4).

The Challenge
Card 6
The Lovers

The bestial couple of the previous Trump is a corrupted version of the beauteous pair illustrated here. A Major Arcana card in this spread position represents a hitherto unexplored motivating force capable of altering the Trend Flow (Card 5) produced by the basic conflict (Cards 1 and 2). Continuing the idea of the couple as divergent aspects of the individual reader, The Lovers proposed ending the negative trend through harmonious integration. The Challenge would involve recognizing the known (Cards 1 and 2) and unknown portions (Card 3) of the conflict, taking responsibility for those capable of being changed (Cards 4 and 5), and then acting constructively toward the desired goal. Recognizing failure as a possibility, the reader was able to compare disappointment with the then current trend and the well-balanced outcome offered by The Lovers. Ultimately, only the reader can determine if the risk of accepting The Challenge outweighs the option of continuing the Trend Flow (Card 5).

Summary

The reading was productive in identifying the source of the conflict (Cards 1 and 2) and illustrating its connection to the dissatisfying phase (Card 5) experienced. In its most general sense, this inability to accomplish certain goals (Card 5) was linked to the reader's self-doubt (Card 1) and impatience (Card 4). The reader's aspirations (Card 3) were strong enough to motivate change and acted as the impetus for the reading itself. Finally, the reading provided an optimal vision of accomplishing goals through a reasonable and responsible approach (Card 6).

During the course of an open reading such as this one, the reader may comprehend specific details related to the subject under exploration. Yet then again, the reader may not. Regardless, you should not approach the session in the role of master-sleuth determined to unravel your own mystery. Instead, a vastly more productive perspective is one motivated by a wish to gain self-understanding through the dynamic reading experience. Uncovering the cards' messages and their relationships within the particular spread in a clear and concise manner is the primary method of achieving this. Undoubtedly, this requires some degree of self-confidence and faith in the reading process itself to provide what you need. Quite often, a session's full import is not realized fully immediately afterwards, but blossoms via further contemplation over time.

Soul of the Matter
6-card spread
Purpose: To encourage transformation through conflict resolution.

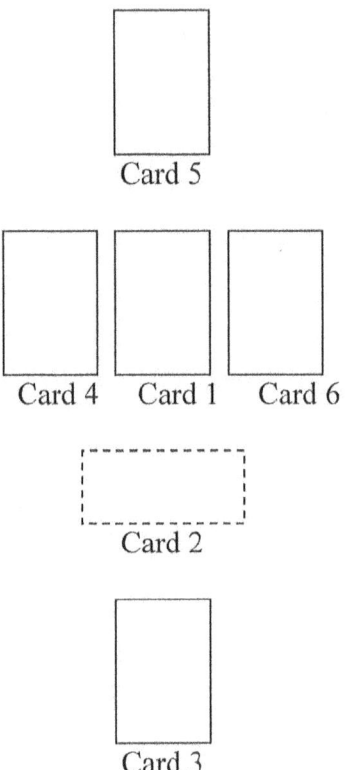

This spread is a variation on the previously explored Heart of the Matter. As such, it uses six cards, works well in assessing a conflict while providing a resolution suggestion, and includes Shadow and Trend Flow cards. While the layout is the same for both spreads, the difference here is in viewing all of the figures in each card as direct representations of the self. In this way, a more precise tracking of your transformative evolvement across time can take place.

If a card shows more than one figure, such a group can represent positive or negative interaction between various aspects of you in the matter under exploration. Adhering to this method can prove revelatory in its implications. As for cards incorporating animals or non-human forms, interpret their symbolism as also signifying you. In this way, a single card provides an even greater depth of information. This method is usable with any of the spreads offered here.

Refer to the section on meanings of the card positions for the Heart of the Matter spread since they are the same used here. As an additional illuminating exercise, the learner is encouraged to interpret the same six cards using the Heart of the Matter and Soul of the Matter approaches separately.

Place Card 2 horizontally across Card 1 during the initial laying out of the cards. Then turn Card 2 upright to the right-hand side of Card 1 during the reading process. Determine additional messages by completing this assessment with Card 2 placed to the left-hand side of Card 1.

Sample Self-Reading
Reading Purpose: an open reading

Interpretation
Overview

Immediately apparent in the Major and Minor cards drawn were recurring themes centered on the reader's growing awareness causing discord with a group. Further issues of burden and release indicated a difficult conflict requiring potentially disruptive action for its resolution. It would remain the reader's decision whether to continue with the trend indicated or to accept a challenge toward change.

Key Aspect
Card 1
The Sun

In this spread position, a Major Arcana card represents the key motivating force causing the conflict. With the reader as the enlightened child of The Sun, the figure's symbolic youth indicated a recent awareness of a significant issue. Furthermore, viewing the galloping horse as the reader as well illustrated how rapidly this consciousness came into being.

Key Opposition or Reinforcement
Card 2
Page of Cups

The Court figure's fixation on the cup illustrated the key situation causing the core imbalance of the conflict through reinforcement of the Trump (Card 1). The Page being older than The Sun's child (Card 1) signaled the reader's continued obsession with the conflict moving forward in time. Even so, their relative closeness in age denoted the reader's childlike sense of vulnerability to the conflict. The suit itself hinted at the emotional upset invested in the situation. The reader as simultaneously the fish and Page demonstrated, respectively, a total immersion in the conflict and the resultant self-scrutiny it caused. As a result, the reader learned something significant about the self.

Shadow
Card 3
Ten of Wands

This Pip defined the Shadow situation manifesting the conflict. The reader interpreted it as one previously blocked until recently revealed as evidenced by the very nature of the conflict and its reinforcement (Cards 1 and 2). The Ten of Wands illustrates this burden of knowledge metaphorically. The backbreaking weight of this situation consumed every area of the reader's existence. It rendered the reader unable to see ahead in the same way as the card's struggling figure, blinded by the bundle of wands. The reader's acknowledgement of the situation's all-consuming impact prompted awareness (Card 1) and a need for change explored in the session.

What Already Possess or Experienced
Card 4
Ten of Cups

The Pip's joyous scene illustrated the reader's past experience contributing to the present conflict. The reader chose one of the children as representative. In light of the conflict, the figure's joyousness was one possible perhaps only though ignorance of a difficult truth. Sometimes, as in the present reading, this spread position assists in clarifying the source of the conflict (Card 1). Here, the Pip's theme pointed toward this source as originating from within the reader's family or support group. The relevant suit reiterated the profound emotional resonance of the conflict already encountered (Card 2) in the reading.

Trend Flow
Card 5
Five of Swords

In this spread position, the cruel situation illustrated by the Five of Swords characterized the most likely outcome of the conflict. Conceivably, the growing self-awareness already described (Card 1) jeopardized the reader's position in the unit. Compounding this risk was the threat of public exposure of the group's internal problem (Card 4). Here, cast as one of the retreating figures, the reader became the target of some form of treachery initiated by the scene's victor, a member of the group (Card 4). The obvious disparity between the deceptively idyllic scene from the past (Card 4) and this potentially menacing one indicated a dramatic change.

The Challenge
Card 6
Ace of Cups

An Ace in this spread position presents the basic realm, yet unexplored, capable of altering the negative Trend Flow (Card 5). The hand position depicted is not only one of giving, but also that of an adult. The reader interpreted this card as the challenge to explore the nurturing realm characterized by the suit of Cups. As already implied, a significant aspect of such an undertaking would call for the acceptance of uneasy truths about others and the self, while perhaps disturbing the status quo (Cards 1 and 5). The reader understood how with a nurturing hand, this accomplishment may very well lead to positive progress. More specifically, the Pip's constructive attributes of acting benevolently without defensiveness would produce the best outcome. That the Ace featured the hand of an adult in contrast to the child figures of the others drawn (Cards 1, 2, and 4) showed maturation to result. Elaborating upon this idea, the reader noted how the risk of accepting the challenge described here might require the releasing of past securities. To illustrate this, the reader imagined the child representative (Card 4) letting go of the hands of the other youth.

Summary

The most significant purpose of this open reading was not in revealing the particulars of the reader's conflict with the group. Instead, recognition of the conflict and willingness to alter it for the better became of more importance. While the possible risks involved in the latter were quite real, the reader believed them worthwhile in resolving the conflict.

IV
Where All Paths Meet

May my heart increase. May it open wide as sky, enough to hold the breadth of god.
—Normandi Ellis, *Awakening Osiris: A New Translation of the Egyptian Book of the Dead*[2]

---

72 Ellis, *Awakening Osiris.*

Returning to the Open Road

There are several techniques useful in bringing closure to a successful and satisfying self-reading. While attempting any of the previous spreads, you may sometimes encounter occasional instances in which the cards' messages are not satisfactorily clear. In such cases and with discretion, you may choose to draw additional cards for clarification. This procedure is best after a thorough analysis of all the cards already drawn for the spread. Attempt to use no more than three additional individual cards or grouping of three cards in total for a particular spread position or level. Neither is it recommended to carry out this optional step for more than three separate spread positions or levels per reading. Adding more than what is suggested here would most likely complicate such further explorations unnecessarily. No extra shuffling or cutting is required before the removal of such cards from the remainder of the previously used deck.

During the session's closing stages, you may still perceive a sense of uncertainty as to how to proceed in light of the reading's messages. You might remove a single, overall guidance card from the remaining deck. This option may be utilized whether additional clarification cards are drawn or not. During this process, consider the most salient aspects of the card drawn. Then contemplate these into terms of suggested action in line with the overall reading. This method is of particular relevancy to spreads analyzing a conflict and its resolution.

Now incorporate all of the reading's messages into a summing up of the entire session. During this grand overview, focus on the central messages of each card or card grouping. Make special note of the deeper messages uncovered through the interrelationships between them and, depending on the spread, its different levels. This may include determining more fully the reading's outcome, options to achieving conflict resolution, and sought after alterations to undesirable trends.

Always be assured of how you possess an active and decisive role in each of these potentialities.

As a final step, gather all of the cards drawn for the session into a single pile. Then, one by one, place each card face-up in an upright position upon the reading surface. Then group the cards according to theme. It is most constructive to limit these to no more than three common categories. While experimenting with and tailoring them to the focus of the session, especially productive groupings can include, but are not limited to: one concerning the "revealed" aspects of the imbalance or issue explored, another relating to the "veiled" aspects and how their understanding can assist in overcoming imbalance, and then perhaps a final set articulating the reading's most significant messages and the resolution of the area examined. This technique frees the cards from their spread positions and levels in order to view them with a fresh perspective. This method works best with spreads using six cards.

Once any final messages are received, gather up the cards into a single pile to shuffle and cut them as before. Three repetitions of the shuffling and cutting steps are sufficient. Besides randomly rearranging the deck in a thorough manner, this closing act provides a visible conclusion to the entire experience.

Intuitive Knowing

The taking of unexpected alternative routes enriches any path. So at least on the surface, there would seem little in common between the Tarot and music. However, students of either excel by developing creative sensitivity, a pioneer willingness to explore innermost realms, and an intuitive trusting in the self.

In his 18th-century treatise on keyboard performance, C.P.E. Bach,[73]

---

73 Carl Philipp Emanuel Bach was born in Weimar, Germany in 1714 and died in Hamburg, Germany in 1788.

a son of composer Johann Sebastian Bach, recommends the use of "good taste" in all musicianship. Although what is perplexing for the learner is his canny refusal to either define this elusive ability, or specify all the needed measures to find it. Perhaps the musical genius knew these answers often manifest themselves through a combination of thoughtful instruction, sincere effort, and artistic experimentation. For their source can be found within the individual provided a genuine commitment exists. Students of the Tarot are able to make the same discovery. For them, the concept of "good taste" may include sound reading practices and brave introspection.

Popular culture encourages the belief that Tarot readers possess a highly developed psychic ability to foretell specific future events through the cards. While it would be limiting to discredit those making similar claims, most practitioners are uninterested in promising the delivery of such an arguably divine feat. Instead, many self-readers are rightfully satisfied with the considerable challenge of seeking self-guidance through the cards and an acceptance of an active role in their own destinies. On the snares and boons of divination, Philip Carr-Gomm and Richard Heygate advise:

> Although using the Tarot for prediction might at first sight seem tempting, ultimately it will sap you of power—because it will lead you to act as if your life were determined solely by outside forces. Instead you need to use the Tarot as a means of gaining insight into the hidden dynamics of a situation or your soul. Then it will do the opposite—it will give you a sense of power and control over your life. It will increase your self-knowledge and as a result lead you closer to that goal of the magical art: wisdom.[74]

The undeniable function of your intuitive sense will become

---

74 Philip Carr-Gomm and Richard Heygate, *The Book of English Magic* (London, 2009).

increasingly apparent as you gain experience, especially during practice sessions. For from them, countless questions arise. The following is just a small sampling. Which card interpretations among potentially many should you focus upon—regardless of what a spread position dictates? When deciphering a Court card with a broader scope, how do you decide if it signifies yourself, another individual, a situation, or an action? If an outcome is overridingly negative in tone, what is the most constructive method of embracing this information?

Valid responses to these questions are myriad. This is so since choices in this process and personal style reflect more than your Tarot studies alone. Knowledge of unrelated areas and the breadth of your life experience intrinsically influence these as well. So then, the quality and variety of every aspect of daily existence—from the mundane to the spiritual—contribute to your self-reading experience.

As regular practice with the Tarot progresses, you will increasingly encounter readings of a consistently potent nature. It would be inaccurate to attribute this experience to supernatural powers possessed by the deck itself. Instead, as proficiency is gained, the cards' messages and those derived from their multitude of combinations become ever more apparent—their secret language revealed.[75] This is the dawning of intuitive knowing, an awesome harmony between your mind, heart, spirit, and the unknown. It is the ability to perceive and make sense of those vital links between the everyday and numinous worlds—those that give existence deeper meaning. During the self-reading process, the cards

---

75 Andrew D. Chumbley, *Qutub* (Chelmsford, 1995). In this book, the author addresses the concept of *Sandyabhasa* (variously spelled Sanskrit term, including sāṅdhyābhāṣā), defined as a "hidden speech of intent" or "twilight language" by which comprehension of the esoteric depths of verbal, non-verbal, and visual communication is a reliant upon progressive training and experience.

manifest these connections in ways not readily discernible by the inexperienced practitioner. A worthwhile session happens when the musician-like reader interprets them into a soaring aria of genuine practical use and mystical depth.

As explained early, the Rider-Waite Tarot has been employed in this guide due to its undeniable importance and influence on innumerable decks worldwide for more than a century. Yet there may come a moment in your ongoing relationship with the cards when you seek out another. Author and spiritual instructor Mélusine Draco addresses the need to locate a deck through which mystical communication is possible:

> The choice of Tarot deck is of the utmost importance. In simple terms, the design of the Major Arcana needs to communicate directly with our soul. If a deck is chosen merely because it is pretty or "nice" then it reveals a certain triviality of spirit; a deck chosen because the cards "speak" to us on an intuitive level is the one that will gradually open up the doors to knowledge, wisdom and understanding. At first we may not fully understand the "language"—which is often at odds to that given in the accompanying handbooks—but with practice we find ourselves entering into realms we only thought existed in our imagination.[76]

You may be concerned with the level of responsibility accepted for subsequent action taken based upon a self-reading. Arguments exist supporting how the source of intuited messages resides in, among other areas, the metaphysical, the psychological, the academic, or any combination of these. The comprehension of this is a highly individualistic one and the result of ongoing study and practice. As already suggested for the outset of a session, intend that what might be acted upon from such messages will be for the greater good of all.

Insisting on absolutely conclusive direction from a reading is most

---

76 Mélusine Draco, correspondence with author, August 2016.

often futile for that is not its most beneficial function. Referring here to self-understanding, the 11th-century Persian Sufi philosopher Al-Ghazâlî[77] articulates the basic concerns at the core of the mostly commonly made queries of the divination process:

> Real self-knowledge consists in knowing the following things: What are you in yourself and where did you come from? Where are you going and for what purpose are you tarrying here awhile? In what does your real happiness and misery consist?[78]

When the Tarot casts light where it is most needed, blinders blocking options capable of balancing your life are lifted. It is through an exploratory self-reading that the reasons so often sought are found. Learning the basics of the methods offered here will build confidence, provide the foundation upon which improvisation can happen, and allow divination to become an art form. To be sure, patience and discipline are needed in what can become ceaseless training. The mystic Sri Ramakrishna[79] welcomed the eternal role of pupil when stating, "As long as I live, so long do I learn."[80] Replacing the need "to be right" or to dictate "what is correct" with an egoless faith in the creative process will allow divination to fulfill its potential as an art form. Over time, the cards will act as mystical portals through which deeper truth can be accessed.

---

77 Al-Ghazâlî was born in Tûs, Iran in 1058 where he died in 1111.
78 Fadiman and Frager, eds., *Essential Sufism* (San Francisco, 1997).
79 Ramakrishna (born Gadadhar Chattopadhyaya) was born in Kamarpukur, India in 1836 and died in Cossipore, India in 1886.
80 Ramakrishna, *Sayings of Sri Ramakrishna: The Most Exhaustive Collection of Them, Their Number Being 1120.* (Madras, 1949). The following book offers a detailed account of the 19th-century Indian mystic's life: M. (Mahendranath Gupta), Swami Nikhilananda, trans., *The Gospel of Ramakrishna* (New York, 1942).

Incorporating divination into a well-tempered life as a way to expand vision is a worthwhile goal. Ultimately though, nothing can transform and elevate one's insight more than opening our hearts to life. Perhaps Hazrat Inayat Khan's words can speak to us about that moment when we put the cards down and direct our glance outward with love:

> ...once one begins to know the heart life is a continual phenomenon, every moment of life becomes a miracle...and all things become so clear to him that he does not ask for any greater phenomenon or miracle: it is a miracle in itself.[81]

Centuries ago, but still several after the appearance of the first Tarot decks, C.P.E. Bach advised the novice musician, "Play from the soul, not like a trained bird!"[82] So to the Tarot apprentice and master alike, let us relate this same directive to our own work with these seventy-eight cards of endless enchantment. In pursuing this shared goal, let us recognize the need for patience and discipline in our endless development. Grant us the vision to perceive most fully the Tarot's profound teachings and the capacity to receive its messages in a meaningful way. And provide us with a spirit fearless of the mysterious transformations to happen within.

---

81   Barks and Khan, *The Hand of Poetry*.
82   Carl Philipp Emanuel Bach, William J. Mitchell, trans., *Essay on the True Art of Playing Keyboard Instruments, Part One, 1753, Part Two, 1762* (New York, 1949).

Beyond the Inner Path

Go then and make of the world something beautiful, set up a light in the darkness.
—Normandi Ellis, *Awakening Osiris: A New Translation of the Egyptian Book of the Dead* [83]

Just as the Fool's journey, no reading is ever truly finished. And the moment of glory enjoyed by the resplendent entity depicted at the center of The World is a fleeting one at best. Reborn anew through the Tarot's often thrilling and sometimes demanding, yet always illuminating experience, the figure has become the Fool once more, re-entering life with an expanded vision, even if returning to the novice level. So in the end is the beginning on this cyclical passage of transformation. The same is so for all of us since the learning process is never completed. For the true challenge of those enlightened is to apply the wisdom gained on each repetition of the quest to the experience of everyday life. In this way, all planes of existence are revealed and unified to achieve the following describing such a mystical state, "He Whose centre is everywhere and Whose circumference nowhere."[84]

In the preceding text, I hope to provide a practical, yet heart-expanding foundation on the art of self-reading with the Tarot. Naturally, this work does not purport to be definitive in any way. There is a wealth of extraordinary materials flourishing by more learned comrades during the occult renaissance we are enjoying today. This little book is simply

---

83   Ellis, *Awakening Osiris*.
84   Chumbley, *Qutub*. Variations of this philosophical paradox have been attributed to a wide-range of mystics across time, including Empedocles, Giordano Bruno, and Aleister Crowley, among others. Learn more in the following book: Finley Eversole, Ph.D., *Art and Spiritual Transformation: The Seven Stages of Death and Rebirth* (Rochester, 2009).

an offering of one approach reflecting its author's development at the time of publication. Most assuredly, my views and reading style will evolve along with further experience in reading the cards and living as fully as I attempt to everyday. *I wish the very same for you!*

At the start of this book, you were urged to *look* at the cards themselves for understanding them. I am making this appeal once more. No level of proficiency should preclude this practice. For no amount of book study, Internet research, or seminar attendance can substitute for it. Above all else, the Tarot reveals its most profound messages in a visual exchange between yourself and the images. What makes the cards especially worthy of continued investigation is how these messages evolve in conjunction with sincere practice and life experience.

Understanding from the outset the impossibility of learning every aspect of the cards is a freeing realization. You can see this recognition in the serenity of The World's central figure—the Fool now illuminated by a deeper wisdom of the heart for a glorious instant before arriving upon the inner path once more.

The 13th-century Persian poet Sa'adi[85] proclaims, "Even the leaves of the tree become as pages of the sacred book once the eyes of the heart are open."[86] Let this describe the moment when the cards are set down. For now your explorations through them will allow you to see well beyond them. Know how the wonder both surrounding and within you is never without joy, challenge, and mystery.

Revelation unfolds within the open heart.

---

85   Sa'adi was born in Shiraz, Iran in 1210 where he died in (approx.) 1291.

86   Hazrat Inayat Khan, *The Alchemy of Happiness* (London, 1996).

Afterword
By Normandi Ellis

Reading a Tarot card to me has always been as exciting a process as reading a hieroglyphic text. When I was learning to read glyphs I came across R.A. Schwaller de Lubicz and his book *Symbol and the Symbolic*. A small tome, it was nonetheless potent in pointing out an obvious and overlooked quality: "Brightness and shadow make light. Without shadow, no object would be visible, so that if brightness were without shadow, we should no more know light than does a blind man."[87]

That is what Michael Orlando Yaccarino's book is—Light, a revelation of life passages writ in brilliance and shadow. I've been a student of Tarot for many years, and have used it for self-reflection and meditation as well as for consultations with others. I believe his insights into the suits and the Pips are as clear and well-thought out as any explanations of the Trumps, which oft receive more contemplation per Tarot book and tend to overshadow the daily life events of the lesser

---

87 R.A. Schwaller de Lubicz, *Symbol and the Symbolic: Ancient Egypt, Science, and the Evolution of Consciousness* (New York, 1981).

cards. We as a culture do that so often, overlook the daily habit of our being in search of the Big Kahuna. This book, bless it and its author, do not do that. As a result, I think I learned a great deal from Michael's narrations of the cards and the balance of the veiled and unveiled meanings.

The placement of the cards for reading is not repetitive, but innovative and quite well-examined. When one is reading for oneself, it is of the utmost importance to resist seeing what is coming (so we can jump up and prepare for it), but rather to see what IS right in front of us, in all its complexity and possibility. And so these readings slow one down long enough to achieve that, long enough to effect a communion between the inner light and the outer form through the medium of the deck.

Thankful Remembrance

This book is a reflection of and adorned by the wisdom, guidance, and artistry of so many. While my associations with them may have begun with distant admiration, I now cherish them as dear friends. I remain grateful to my publisher Chris (Mogg) Morgan whose encouragement and belief in this book brought it to light at last, enhanced by his ancient knowledge. My appreciation extends to everyone at Mandrake of Oxford for their splendid work on this project. For the inimitable Rachel Pollack, whose superlative masterworks on the Tarot—shining with undeniable practicality, depth, and warm humor—remain unparalleled. For Normandi Ellis, whose ever radiant words awakened realization of a spiritual siblinghood. For Enrique Enriquez, who taught me how to perceive the eye's poetic messages. For Mary K. Greer, whose generous suggestions on maximizing the dynamic qualities of the text in a previous manifestation were implemented and her astute comments included throughout. For Paul Huson, who provided constructive comments when this work was in early draft form, and then a sparkling gem for the final version. Truly appreciated contributions were bestowed by the following luminaries, in every sense of the term: Nimue Brown; Mélusine Draco; Gemma Gary; Shani Oates; Alan Richardson; and Julian Vayne, who pointed me toward several essential texts and deeper insights as well. For Nancy Barta-Norton, who shared research materials on the Tarot's connection to Egypt. For Robert Ansell, Fulgur Limited; Jane Cox, Troy Books; and Ashley Mortimer, Doreen Valiente Foundation, who all provided kind assistance. For so many mystics named and unnamed whose work has enriched immeasurably my approach with the cards. For all those who allowed me the privilege of learning my craft through their centers, organizations, and events. For the remarkable artist Gary Lund, whose work sets this soul dancing. For David Palladini, whose vibrantly stunning artwork remains evergreen. For Scot D. Ryersson, an exceptional artist whose elegantly insightful illustrations and continual support have elevated this work to reaches impossible without them. And finally, for all those seen and unseen, known and unknown who have awakened this heart's vision.

Select Bibliography and Suggested Reading

Explore the fascinating history, varied practices, and dynamic perspectives of the Tarot and related areas of study through the following books and those cited in the footnotes.

Brown, Nimue. *Spirituality without Structure: The Power of Finding Your Own Path*. Winchester: Moon Books, 2013.

Carr-Gomm, Philip and Richard Heygate. *The Book of English Magic*. London: John Murray (Publishers), 2009.

Cirlot, J.E. *A Dictionary of Symbols*. New York: Philosophical Library, 1962.

Cooper, J.C. *An Illustrated Encyclopaedia of Traditional Symbols*. London: Thames and Hudson Ltd, 1978.

Crowley, Aleister (The Master Therion). *The Book of Thoth: A Short Essay on the Tarot of the Egyptians, Equinox Vol. III, No. V*. York Beach: Weiser Books, 2000.

Decker, Ronald; Thierry Depaulis; and Michael Dummett. *A Wicked Pack of Cards: The Origins of the Occult Tarot*. New York: St. Martin's Press, 1996.

Draco, Mélusine. *The Dictionary of Magic and Mystery*. Alresford: Moon Books, 2012.

Drury, Nevill. *Inner Visions: Explorations in Magical Consciousness*. London: Arkana Penguin Books Ltd, 1994.

DuQuette, Lon Milo. *Understanding Aleister Crowley's Thoth Tarot*. San Francisco: RedWheel/Weiser, 2003.

Ellis, Normandi. *Awakening Osiris: A New Translation of the Egyptian Book of the Dead*. Grand Rapids: Phanes Press, 1988.

Enriquez, Enrique. *Looking at the Marseilles Tarot: Notes on Tarot's Optical Language*. Colchester: Pro Shop Publishing, 2007.

Fadiman, James and Robert Frager, eds. *Essential Sufism*. San Francisco: HarperSanFrancisco, 1997.

Gary, Gemma. *Traditional Witchcraft: A Cornish Book of Ways*. London: Troy Books, 2014.

Graves, F.D. *The Windows of Tarot*. Dobbs Ferry: Morgan & Morgan, Inc., Publishers, 1973.

Gray, Eden. *The Tarot Revealed: A Modern Guide to Reading the Tarot Cards*. New York: Bell Publishing Company, Inc., 1960.

Greer, Mary K. *Tarot for Yourself: A Workbook for Personal Transformation* (Second Edition). Franklin Lakes: New Page Books, 2002.

Huson, Paul. *Mystical Origins of the Tarot: From Ancient Roots to Modern Usage*. Rochester: Destiny Books, 2004.

Jackson, Nigel Aldcroft and Michael Howard. *The Pillars of Tubal-Cain*. Somerset: Capall Bann, 2000.

Kaplan, Stuart R. *The Encyclopedia of Tarot*. 4 vols. Stamford: U.S. Games Systems, Inc., 2006.

Khan, Hazrat Inayat. *The Alchemy of Happiness*. London: East-West Publications, 1996.

Frisvold, Nicholaj, de Mattos. *Craft of the Untamed: An inspired vision of Traditional Witchcraft*. Oxford: Mandrake of Oxford, 2011.

Morgan, Levannah. *A Witch's Mirror: The Art of Making Magic*. Somerset: Capall Bann Publishing, 2013.

O'Neill, Robert V. *Tarot Symbolism*. Melbourne: Association for Tarot Studies, 2004.

Palladini, David. Interview by Michael Orlando Yaccarino. "Sage of Aquarius: David Palladini and the Art of Being." *Tarosophist International*, 2009, vol. 1, issue 5: 5-32.

Pennick, Nigel. *The Eldritch World*. Earl Shilton: Lear Books, 2006.

Place, Robert M. *The Tarot: History, Symbolism, and Divination*. New York: Jeremy P. Tarcher/Penguin, 2005.

Pollack, Rachel. *Seventy-Eight Degrees of Wisdom: A Book of Tarot* (Revised Edition). San Francisco: Weiser Books, 2007.

Rosengarten, Arthur. *Tarot and Psychology: Spectrums of Possibility*. St. Paul: Paragon House, 2000.

Tweedie, Irina. *Daughter of Fire: A Diary of a Spiritual Training with a Sufi Master* (The Complete Unabridged Edition). Grass Valley: Blue Dolphin Publishing, 1986.

Vaughan-Lee, Llewellyn. *The Paradoxes of Love.* Inverness: The Golden Sufi Center, 1996.

Waite, Arthur Edward. *The Pictorial Key to the Tarot: Being Fragments of a Secret Tradition under the Veil of Divination.* London: W. Rider, 1911.

Walters, J. Donald. *Intuition for Starters: How to Know and Trust Your Inner Guidance.* Nevada City: Crystal Clarity Publishers, 2002.

About the Author

Michael Orlando Yaccarino has read, taught, and written about the Tarot. His unique approach expresses decades of exploration and study. For several years, his column *The Common Reader* offered practical, ethical, and mystical advice for the professional Tarot reader worldwide. In addition, Yaccarino has written extensively on alternative film and unconventional historical figures for many international publications. He is the recipient of degrees in psychology and film studies from New York University and is a graduate of Suluk Academy's heart-centered spiritual training in Sufi mysticism. Yaccarino remains a student and explorer of the hidden realms since childhood. With Scot D. Ryersson, he is co-author of the international best-selling biographies *Infinite Variety: The Life and Legend of the Marchesa Casati* and *The Marchesa Casati: Portraits of a Muse*; the play *Infinite Variety: Portrait of a Muse*; the fairy tale *The Princess of Wax: A Cruel Tale*; as well as co-editor of *Spectral Haunts and Phantom Lovers*, a collection of British ghost stories. Yaccarino lives in the Northeastern United States where he co-directs The Casati Archives. Visit marchesacasati.com to learn more.

About the Contributors

Rachel Pollack (Foreword) is the author of thirty six books of fiction and non-fiction, including: two award-winning novels; a poetry collection; a new translation of Sophocles's *Oedipus Tyrannus* ("Oedipus Rex"), with David Vine; and a series of books about Tarot that have become known around the world. Described many times as "the Bible of Tarot readers," her first Tarot book, *Seventy-Eight Degrees of Wisdom*, has been in print continuously since 1980. Pollack has taught and lectured in the U.S., Canada, Europe, the UK, Australia, New Zealand, and China. She has designed and drawn *The Shining Tribe Tarot*, and worked with artist Robert Place to create *The Burning Serpent Oracle* and most recently *The Raziel Tarot*. Pollack's work has been translated into fourteen languages. Among her more recent books is the novel *The Child Eater*. Until her retirement, Pollack was a senior faculty member of Goddard College's MFA in Creative Writing program. She lives in New York's Hudson Valley. Visit rachelpollack.com to learn more.

Normandi Ellis (Afterword) is the award-winning author of fiction, non-fiction, poetry, and memoir. Among her books are *Awakening Osiris*, a new version of the Egyptian Book of the Dead; *Dreams of Isis*, a spiritual autobiography; *Invoking the Scribes of Ancient Egypt*, a literary tour of Egyptian temples; *Imagining the World into Existence*, a primer of Egyptian magic and consciousness; and *The Union of Isis and Thoth*, an experiential exploration of building and inhabiting the temple within. For more than two decades, she has led sacred pilgrimages throughout Egypt. An ordained Spiritualist minister, clairvoyant medium and astrologer, she resides at Camp Chesterfield, Indiana. Visit normandiellis.com to learn more.

Scot D. Ryersson (cover design and interior illustrations) is a renowned illustrator and graphic artist who has lived and worked in London, Toronto, Sydney, and New York City. He is the recipient of two Art Directors of London Awards and is responsible for acclaimed advertising campaigns for many Academy Award®-winning films. Ryersson is also the author of numerous critiques and essays on film and literature. With Michael Orlando Yaccarino, he has co-authored the critically-acclaimed biographies *Infinite Variety: The Life and Legend of the Marchesa Casati* and *The Marchesa Casati: Portraits of a Muse*; the play *Infinite Variety: Portrait of a Muse*; the fairy tale *The Princess of Wax: A Cruel Tale*; as well co-edited *Spectral Haunts and Phantom Lovers*, a collection of British ghost stories. Ryersson lives in the Northeastern United States where he co-directs The Casati Archives. Visit marchesacasati.com to learn more.

Gary Lund (front-cover art) is an award-winning, widely-exhibited American painter, sculptor, and animation film designer. Born in Los Angeles, he studied painting and illustration there at the Chouinard Art Institute. During the late 1960s and 1970s, Lund was responsible for the production design of several highly-regarded animated films, including *The Point* (1971), songwriter Harry Nilsson's celebrated, Emmy Award®-winning fable of non-conformity; and the Academy Award®-nominated short *The Legend of John Henry* (1974). In 1989, he earned the Benjamin Franklin Award for Excellence for his design and illustration of the book *Life: Before, During and After*. Lund's distinctive work has been featured in such leading publications as *Rolling Stone* and the *Los Angeles Times*. He is also the creator of the Third Eye Oracle, printed privately by the artist. Lund's artwork has been collected in the book *Welcome to Earth: Drawings by Gary Lund* and channeled writings in *Open*. He lives in Silver City, New Mexico. Visit gary-lund.com to learn more.

David Palladini (back-cover art and Afterword Egyptian study) was born in Roteglia, Reggio Emilia, Italy in 1946 and raised in Highland Park, Illinois. He attended Pratt Institute of Art (Brooklyn, New York). Palladini is a book illustrator, artist, photographer, teacher, and author. He is the creator of the Aquarian Tarot, one of the most influential decks of the twentieth century, as well as the New Palladini Tarot. Palladini is the author of *The Journal of an Artist*, a memoir; and co-author of *Painting the Soul: The Tarot Art of David Palladini*. He lives in Newport Beach, California. Visit davidpalladini.com to learn more.

Index

Page numbers in italics refer to footnote citations.

A

Ace. *See* Minor Arcana
   As realm 88
   General characteristics 88
Air. *See* Elements: Air (associations): Swords
Al-Ghazâlî 263
Alchemy 19, *28*
Alliette, Jean-Baptiste *16*
Aquarian Tarot (Tarot deck) 12, *20*
Astrology 19, *28*
Atouts (Trumps) *36*
Atu (Trumps) *36*
Atu of Tahuti (Trumps) *36*

B

Bach, C.P.E. 259, 264
Bach, Johann Sebastian 260
Bakr al-Kalâbâdhî, Abû 23
Boaz (biblical name). *See* Major Arcana: The High Priestess
Bowers, Roy. *See* Cochrane, Robert
Brown, Nimue 24

C

Carr-Gomm, Philip 260
Cartomancy 17
   France 17
   Italy 17
Chakras *28*
Channeling 23
Chattopadhyaya, Gadadhar. *See* Ramakrishna
Chumbley, Andrew D. *261*, *265*
Cochrane, Robert 25
Coins
   Early Tarot deck suit *84*
   Symbol 162
Confucius *28*
Constant, Alphonse Louis. *See* Lévi, Éliphas
Contemplation 14, 18, 22, 29, 31, 32, 35, 38, 39, 58, 64, 125, 181, 190, 193, 194, 195, 251, 267
Correspondences (in Tarot reading) 28, 85
Court card. *See* Minor Arcana
   General characteristics 86
   Multiple appearances (in Tarot reading) 87
Crowley, Aleister *16*, 30, *36*, 85
   Book of Thoth, The *16*, 30, *36*, 86
   Thoth Tarot (Tarot deck) *36*
Cutting deck (in Tarot reading) 196, *197*

D

Dee, Steve 33
Deep Mind 18, 193
   Aspects *17*
Divination 17, 22, 24, 25, 31, 189, 191, 193, 194, 199, 260, 263, 264
Draco, Mélusine 262
Drury, Nevill *37*
Dualism 26, 27, 45, 51, 98, 107

E

Earth. *See* Elements
Egypt *16*, *21*, 26, 27, *36*, *37*, 44, 48, 60, 121
Elements 8, 43, 83, 85
   Air (associations).
      Swords. *See* Minor Arcana: Swords
   Ether (quintessence)
      Major Arcana 162
      Pentagram. *See* Pentagram (symbol)
   Fire (associations).
      Wands. *See* Minor Arcana: Wands
Ellis, Normandi 15, 34, 188, 257,

265, 267, 275
Enriquez, Enrique 194
Etteilla. *See* Alliette, Jean-Baptiste

F

Feild, Reshad 23
Fellowship of the Rosy Cross *18*
Fire. *See* Elements
Five-pointed star (symbol). *See* Pentagram (symbol)
Fortune, Dion *191*
Freemasonry 19
Fries, Jan. *See* Deep Mind: Aspects
Frisvold, Nicholaj, de Mattos 221

G

Game-playing cards
  China 16, 84
  France *17*
  India 16
  Islam 16
  Italy 16
  Persia 16
  Tarot suit equivalents 85
  Western Europe 16, *17*, 84
Gary, Gemma 31
Gematria *28*
Golden Dawn. *See* Hermetic Order of the Golden Dawn
Graves, F.D. 12
Gray, Eden 7, 8, 9
Greer, Mary K. 19

H

Harris, Lady Frieda *36*
Hermes (Greek god) 26, *36*
Hermes Trismegistus 26
Hermetic Order of the Golden Dawn 18, 19, 27, *194*
Hermetica. *See* Hermeticism
Hermeticism 26, 27, 44, 52, 64, 85
Heygate, Richard 260
Houses of Wisdom (Trumps) *36*
Howard, Michael 65
Huson, Paul 17, *18*, 84

I

I Ching *28*
Inayat Khan, Hazrat 22, 30, 199, 264

J

Jackson, Nigel Aldcroft 65
Jesus (biblical) 65
Joachim (biblical name). *See* Major Arcana: The High Priestess
Jodorowsky, Alejandro *194*
Judas Iscariot (biblical) 65

K

Kabbalah 19, *28*
Keys (Trumps) *36*
King 86
King (Court card). *See* Minor Arcana
Knight 86
Knight (Court card). *See* Minor Arcana
Kriyananda, Swami 192

L

Last Judgment (biblical event) 80
Lemniscate (symbol) 42, 56, 83, 174
Lenormand, Madame 18
Lévi, Éliphas *16*
Lund, Gary 24, 276

M

Major Arcana 20, 25, 31, 35–40, 67, 84, 88, 98, 120, 162, 207, 238, 262
  Death 37, 66
  Judgement 38, 80, 120
  Justice 37, 57, 62, 63
  Strength 37, 56, 57, 63, 83
  Temperance 37, 68, 74, 76
  The Chariot 37, 54, 68, 228
  The Devil 38, 70, 208, 249
  The Emperor 37, 48, 68
  The Empress 37, 46, 68, 227
  The Fool 21, 35, *37*, 38, 40, 172, 179
  The Hanged Man 37, 64, 66
  The Hermit 37, 58, 133

The Hierophant 37, 50, 58, 70
The High Priestess 37, 44, 68, 82, 120, 208
The Lovers 37, 52, 70, 121, 122, 249
The Magician 37, 42, 56, 248
The Moon 35, 38, 76, 78, 247
The Star 38, 74, 78
The Sun 38, 78, 254
The Tower 38, 72, 74
The Wheel of Fortune 35, 37, 60, 83
The World *37*, 38, 82, 121, 172, 179, 265, 266
Marseilles style (Tarot deck) *36*, *84*
Meditation 16, 31, 58, 190, 193, *194*, 267
Mercury (Roman god) *36*
Minor Arcana 19, 25, 31, 84, 89, 90, 226, 238
   Cups 20, 84, 85, 111, 124
      Ace of Cups 120, *256*
      Eight of Cups 133, 226
      Five of Cups 127
      Four of Cups 125
      King of Cups 112
      Knight of Cups 116
      Nine of Cups 135
      Page of Cups 118, 254
      Queen of Cups 114
      Seven of Cups 131
      Six of Cups 129
      Ten of Cups 136, *255*
      Three of Cups 123
      Two of Cups 121, 229
   Pentacles 20, 84, 85, 162
      Ace of Pentacles 172
      Eight of Pentacles 183
      Five of Pentacles 177
      Four of Pentacles 176
      King of Pentacles 164
      Knight of Pentacles 168
      Nine of Pentacles 184
      Page of Pentacles 170
      Queen of Pentacles 166
      Seven of Pentacles 181, 248
      Six of Pentacles 179
      Ten of Pentacles 186
      Three of Pentacles 175
      Two of Pentacles 174
   Swords 20, 84, 85, 138
      Ace of Swords 146
      Eight of Swords 157
      Five of Swords 152, 215, 255
      Four of Swords 151
      King of Swords 140
      Knight of Swords 144
      Nine of Swords 159, 227
      Page of Swords 145
      Queen of Swords 142
      Seven of Swords 156
      Six of Swords 154, 214
      Ten of Swords 160
      Three of Swords 149, 247
      Two of Swords 147
   Wands 20, 84, 85, 90
      Ace of Wands 97
      Eight of Wands 107
      Five of Wands 103
      Four of Wands 101
      King of Wands 91
      Knight of Wands 94
      Nine of Wands 108
      Page of Wands 96
      Queen of Wands 93, 213
      Seven of Wands 105
      Six of Wands 104
      Ten of Wands 110, 254
      Three of Wands 99
      Two of Wands 98
Morgan, Chris 36, 37
Morgan, Levannah 85
Moses (biblical) 22
Mysticism 25, 35
   Definition *21*

N

Numerology 19, *28*

O

Oates, Shani 189
Occult 7, 12, 16, 20, 28, 31, 36
Odin (Norse god) *65*
Oracles 36
    Oracle deck 16, 18
Ouroboros (symbol) 42
Ouspensky, P.D. *16*

P

Page (Court card). *See* Minor Arcana
Palladini, David 12, *20*, 28, 29, 277
Paranormal experiences (author) 13–14
Péladan, Joséphin *16*
Pennick, Nigel 199
Pentagram (symbol) 162
Pips (Ace-Ten) 10, 20, 84, 85, 87, 88
    Origin *20*, 84
Pixie. *See* Smith, Pamela Colman
Pollack, Rachel 7, 275
Position (card). *See* Spreads (in Tarot reading)

Q

Queen 86
Queen (Court card). *See* Minor Arcana

R

Ram Dass 35
Ramakrishna 263
Revealed message (concept) 31
Reversals (in Tarot reading) 197, 198
Richardson, Alan 88, 89
Rider-Waite (Tarot deck) 19, 20, 27, *36*, 39, 57, 63, 84, 262
Rider-Waite-Smith (Tarot deck). *See* Rider-Waite (Tarot deck)
Roman, Sanaya 23
Rosicrucianism 19
Runes 24, *28*

S

Sa'adi 266
Schwaller de Lubicz, R.A. 267
Self-reading 10, 11, 12, 22, 29, 31, 33, 35, 38, 189, 190, 191, 194, 195, 199, 200, 201, 202, 216, 258, 261, 262, 263, 265
    Sample 207, 213, 226, 246, 253
Shadow (concept) 239, 240
Shemyaza (Persian fallen angel) *65*
Shuffling deck (in Tarot reading) 196, 197
Smith, Pamela Colman 9, 18, 19
Sola-Busca Tarot (Tarot Deck) *84*
Spare, Austin Osman 239
Spreads (custom)
    1-card spread
        Assessment 203
    2-card spread
        Imbalance I.D. 205
    3-card spread
        Present-Past-Future 210
    4-card spread
        Trend Flow 217
    5-card spread
        Arch Bridge 231
        Crossroads 221
    6-card spread
        Guidance 235
        Heart of the Matter 241
        Soul of the Matter 252
Spreads (in Tarot reading) 10, 87, 198–202
Sufis *21*, 22, 23, 30, 263
Suits (Tarot deck). *See* Minor Arcana

T

Tagore, Rabindranath 199, 200
Tahuti (Egyptian god). *See* Thoth (Egyptian god)
Tarocchi (Italian card game) 17, 35
Tarot (term origin). *See* Tarocchi (Italian card game)
Tarot deck (early) 16, 17
    France 17
    Italy 16, *84*
Thoth (Egyptian god) 26, *36*

Thoth Tarot (Tarot deck). *See* Crowley, Aleister
Thrice-Greatest Hermes. *See* Hermes Trismegistus
Tree of Life *28*
Trend Flow (concept) 210–215, 241
Trinick, John B. *18*
Trionfi. *See* Trumps
Parade (medieval Europe) 36, 234
Trumps. *See* Major Arcana
Tweedie, Irina 22

U
Underhill, Evelyn *21*

V
Valiente, Doreen 29

Vaughan-Lee, Llewellyn 190, 197
Vayne, Julian 193
Veiled message (concept) 32
Venus (symbol) 46

W
Waite, Arthur Edward 7, 18, 19
Walters, James Donald. *See* Kriyananda, Swami
Water. *See* Elements
Windows of Tarot, The. *See* Graves, F.D.
Wirth, Oswald *16*
Witchcraft 29, 31

Z
Zodiac *28*

Celestial Arcana
Precession, Tarot & the Secret Doctrine
Titus Salmon
978-1-906958-80-0 £30/$45
SPECIAL HARDCOVER 400 PP

This book is an in-depth study of Tarot symbolism that explores the Arcana's mythology and how it relates to the phenomenon of precession and the Secret Doctrine of Aeonic succession. Much of the symbolism is shown to have been derived from ancient Egyptian, Celtic, Hellenistic, and medieval customs, rituals, and myths, which are traced at least as far back as the Age of Taurus (c. 4200-2100 BCE).

Deeper Into the Underworld
Christopher Allaun 978-1-906958-76-3 £12.99/$US22

Praise for Vol I: Shamanism, Myth, & Magick "...a masterpiece. Chris has thoughtfully taken a huge subject and separated it into readable and manageable sections and chapters. He clarifies – What is the Underworld? Who resides in the Underworld? Where is the Underworld? and Why does it exist?" — all questions that have fascinated mankind since the beginning of time. And Mr. Allaun gives the reader exercises to deal

with the dark side of the underworld, practical ways to cope with exploring one's own fears and terrors, along with ways to help others. He also includes an extensive bibliography, something very useful. From psychologists to ceremonial magicians to spirit workers, to people just trying to navigate today's complex world, Underworld creates a clear path full of information and help, to guide us through these often troubling times. I highly recommend this book!"- Janet Barres

www.ingramcontent.com/pod-product-compliance
Lightning Source LLC
Chambersburg PA
CBHW060833190426
43197CB00039B/2573